D1486799

THE RAINTREE
ILLUSTRATED
SCIENCE
ENCYCLOPEDIA.

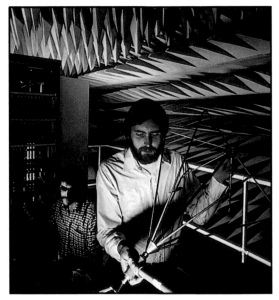

VOLUME 1
AAR-ART

RAINTREE
STECK-VAUGHN
L I B R A R Y
A Division of Steck-Vaughn Company

Managing Editors

Corinn Codye
Writer and editor of social science
    and science textbooks
Paul Q. Fuqua
Writer and editor of films, filmstrips,
    and books on scientific subjects

Raintree Editorial

Barbara J. Behm, Editor
Elizabeth Kaplan, Editor
Lynn M. Marcinkowski, Project Editor
Judith Smart, Editor-in-Chief

Raintree Art/Production

Suzanne Beck, Art Director
Kathleen A. Hartnett, Designer
Carole Kramer, Designer
Eileen Rickey, Typesetter
Andrew Rupniewski, Production Manager

Copyright © 1991 Steck-Vaughn Company

Text copyright © 1991, Raintree Publishers Limited Partnership

For photographic credits, see Volume 18

Drawn art copyright © 1991, 1984, 1979 Macdonald Children's
Books (A Division of Simon & Schuster Young Books) and Raintree
Publishers Limited Partnership

Library of Congress Number: 90-40559

Library of Congress Cataloging-in-Publication Data

The Raintree illustrated science encyclopedia.
    Includes bibliographical references and index.

    Summary: Presents principles, concepts, and people in the various fields of
science and technology.
    1. Science—Encyclopedias, Juvenile.   2. Technology—
Encyclopedias, Juvenile.   [1. Science—Encyclopedias.   2. Technology—
Encyclopedias.   3. Encyclopedias and dictionaries.]   I. Raintree Publishers.
Q121.R34   1991   90-40559
503—dc20   CIP
ISBN 0-8172-3800-X (set)   AC
ISBN 0-8172-3801-8 (Volume 1)

Cover photo: See page 96.
Title page photo: See page 16.

2 3 4 5 6 7 8 9 10   95 94 93 92 91

General Science:
Dr. Glenn D. Berkheimer (G.D.B.)
Michigan State University

Dr. Geoffrey C. Crockett (G.C.C.)
Aldrich Chemical Company, Inc.

Geology:
Dr. William R. Shirk (W.R.S.)
Shippensburg State College

Herpetology:
Dr. Charles J. Cole (C.J.C.)
American Museum of Natural
    History

Richard L. Lattis (R.L.L.)
New York Zoological Society

Ichthyology:
Edward C. Migdalski (E.C.M.)
Outdoor Education Center,
    Yale University

Industrial Science:
Edith H. Gladden (E.H.G.)
Philadelphia Regional Introduction
    of Minorities to Engineering

F. Joseph Merlino (F.J.M.)
Philadelphia Renaissance in Science
    and Math

Lower Invertebrates:
Dr. Carl S. Hammen (C.S.H.)
University of Rhode Island

Mammalogy:
Dr. John J. Mayer (J.J.M.)
University of Connecticut

Mathematics:
Sarvendra P. Agarwal (S.P.A.)
Rensselaer Polytechnic Institute

Dr. Robert J. Sovchik (R.J.S.)
University of Akron

Medicine/Anatomy:
Dr. Leslie V. Cohen (L.V.C.)
University of Michigan

Dr. James J. Ferguson (J.J.F.)
School of Medicine, University of
    Pennsylvania

Dr. Moss H. Mendelson (M.H.M.)
University of Colorado Health
    Sciences Center

Mineralogy:
Dr. Robert Hamilton (R.H.)
Colorado School of Mines

Nutrition:
Dr. Leslie O. Schulz (L.O.S.)
University of Wisconsin-Milwaukee

Optics:
Dr. Stanley S. Ballard (S.S.B.)
University of Florida

Ornithology:
Mary LeCroy (M.L.)
American Museum of Natural
    History

Dr. Lawrence L. Rauch (L.L.R.)
California Institute of Technology

Dr. Lester L. Short (L.L.S.)
California Institute of Technology

Paleontology:
Diane L. Gabriel (D.L.G.)
Milwaukee Public Museum

Physical Science:
Dr. John Daintith (J.D.)
Aylesbury, England, author,
    Introducing Science

Kathleen A. Gustavson (K.A.G.)
Nicolet Public High School

Dr. Alan Isaacs (A.I.)
Aylesbury, England, author,
    Dictionary of Physical Sciences

Dr. Ernest W. Lee (E.W.L.)
University of North Carolina at
    Greensboro

Dr. James Tucci (J.T.)
University of Bridgeport

Dr. Edward D. Walton (E.D.W.)
California State Polytechnic
    University

Dr. Louis Winkler (L.W.)
Pennsylvania State University

Radiological Science:
American College of Radiology
    (A.C.R.)

Rocketry/Aeronautics:
Jesco von Puttkamer (J.vP.)
Office of Space Transportation
    Systems

Science Units:
Dr. Richard W. Lindquist (R.W.L.)
Wesleyan University

USING THE RAINTREE ILLUSTRATED SCIENCE ENCYCLOPEDIA

You are living in a world in which science, technology, and nature are very important. You see something about science almost every day. It might be on television, in the newspaper, in a book at school, or some other place. Often, you want more information about what you see. *The Raintree Illustrated Science Encyclopedia* will help you find what you want to know. The Raintree encyclopedia has information on many science subjects. You may want to find out about mathematics, biology, agriculture, the environment, computers, or space exploration, for example. They are all in *The Raintree Illustrated Science Encyclopedia*. There are many, many other subjects covered as well.

There are eighteen volumes in the encyclopedia. The articles, which are called entries, are in alphabetical order through the first seventeen volumes. On the spine of each volume, below the volume number, are some letters. The letters above the line are the first three letters of the first entry in that volume. The letters below the line are the first three letters of the last entry in that volume. In Volume 1, for example, you see that the first entry begins with **aar** and that the last entry begins with **art**. Using the letters makes it easy to find the volume you need.

In Volume 18, there are interesting projects that you can do on your own. The projects are fun to do, and they illustrate important science principles. Also in Volume 18, there are two special features—an index and a bibliography.

Main Entries. The titles of the main entries in *The Raintree Illustrated Science Encyclopedia* are printed in capital letters. They look like this: **CAMERA**. At the beginning of most entries, you will see a phonetic pronunciation of the entry title. In the front of each volume, there is a pronunciation key. Use it the same way you use your dictionary's pronunciation key.

At the end of each entry, there are two sets of initials. They often look like this: P.Q.F./J.E.P. The first set belongs to the person or persons who wrote the entry. The second set belongs to the special consultant or consultants who checked the entry for accuracy. Pages iii and iv in Volume 1 give you the names of all these people.

Cross-References. Sometimes, a subject has two names. The Raintree encyclopedia usually puts the information under the more common name. However, in case you look up the less common name, there will be a cross-reference to tell you where to find the information. Suppose you wanted to look up something about the metric temperature scale. This scale is usually called the Celsius Scale. Sometimes, however, it is called the Centigrade Scale. The Raintree encyclopedia has the entry **CELSIUS SCALE**. If you looked up Centigrade Scale, you would find this: **CENTIGRADE SCALE** *See* CELSIUS SCALE. This kind of cross-reference tells you where to find the information you need.

There is another kind of cross-reference in the Raintree encyclopedia. It looks like this: *See* CLOUD. Or it looks like this: *See also* ELECTRICITY. These cross-references tell you where to find other helpful information on the subject you are reading about.

Projects. At the beginning of some entries, you will see this symbol: **PROJECT** It tells you that there is a project related to that entry in Volume 18.

Illustrations. There are thousands of photographs, graphs, diagrams, and tables in the Raintree encyclopedia. They will help you better understand the entries you read. Captions describe the illustrations. Many of the illustrations also have labels that point out important parts.

Index. The index lists every main entry by volume and page number. Many subjects that are not main entries are also listed in the index.

Bibliography. In Volume 18, there is also a bibliography for students. The books in this list are on a variety of topics and can supplement what you have learned in the Raintree encyclopedia.

The Raintree Illustrated Science Encyclopedia was designed especially for you, the young reader. It is a source of knowledge for the world of science, technology, and nature. Enjoy it.

PRONUNCIATION KEY

Each symbol has the same sound as the darker letters in the sample words.

ə	balloon, ago	i	rip, ill	sh	shoot, machine
ər	learn, further	ī	side, sky	t	to, stand
a	map, have	j	join, germ	th	thin, death
ā	day, made	k	king, ask	t̪h	then, this
ä	father, car	l	let, cool	ü	pool, lose
aů	now, loud	m	man, same	ů	put, book
b	ball, rib	n	no, turn	v	view, give
ch	choose, nature	ng	bring, long	w	wood, glowing
d	did, add	ō	cone, know	y	yes, year
e	bell, get	ȯ	all, saw	z	zero, raise
ē	sweet, easy	ȯi	boy, boil	zh	leisure, vision
f	fan, soft	p	part, scrap	'	strong accent
g	good, big	r	root, tire	'	weak accent
h	hurt, ahead	s	so, press		

GUIDE TO MEASUREMENT ABBREVIATIONS

All measurements in *The Raintree Illustrated Science Encyclopedia* are given in both the customary, or English, system and the metric system [in brackets like these]. Following are the abbreviations used for various units of measure.

Customary Units of Measure

mi. = miles	cu. yd. = cubic yards
m.p.h. = miles per hour	cu. ft. = cubic feet
yd. = yards	cu. in. = cubic inches
ft. = feet	gal. = gallons
in. = inches	pt. = pints
sq. mi. = square miles	qt. = quarts
sq. yd. = square yards	lb. = pounds
sq. ft. = square feet	oz. = ounces
sq. in. = square inches	fl. oz. = fluid ounces
cu. mi. = cubic miles	°F. = degrees Fahrenheit

Metric Units of Measure

km = kilometers	cu. km = cubic kilometers
kph = kilometers per hour	cu. m = cubic meters
m = meters	cu. cm = cubic centimeters
cm = centimeters	ml = milliliters
mm = millimeters	kg = kilograms
sq. km = square kilometers	g = grams
sq. m = square meters	mg = milligrams
sq. cm = square centimeters	°C = degrees Celsius

For information on how to convert customary measurements to metric measurements, see the **METRIC SYSTEM** article in Volume 10.

A

AARDVARK (ärd′värk′) The aardvark is an African mammal of the family Orycteropodidae. (*See* MAMMAL.) The aardvark is found from Ethiopia to South Africa. *Aardvark* means "earth pig" in the Afrikaans language. The aardvark is about the size of a pig. It has a long snout. Its tongue can be extended 18 in. [45 cm]. Aardvarks range in color from dull brownish gray to sandy yellow.

Aardvarks are nocturnal, which means they are active at night. They use their sharp claws to dig into ant and termite hills. With their long tongues, they scoop up and eat the insects.　　　　　　　　　　S.R.G./J.J.M.

AARDWOLF (ärd′wŭlf′) The aardwolf is an African mammal that belongs to the family Hyaenidae. (*See* MAMMAL.) This uncommon animal is found from South Africa to Angola.

Although it resembles a hyena, the aardwolf is much smaller. It grows to only 30 in. [75 cm] in length. The fur of the aardwolf is grayish yellow with black markings. Aardwolves spend their days in underground holes. They come out at night to hunt small animals, including termites, their major source of food. *See also* HYENA.　　　　　S.R.G./J.J.M.

ABACUS (ab′ə kəs) An abacus is a device once widely used for counting and doing arithmetic. The abacus probably was invented thousands of years ago in the Middle East and then spread throughout Asia. An abacus is

The aardvark's sharp claws are well suited for digging. It captures termites and ants with its long tongue.

made of a wooden frame with beads strung on wires stretched between two of its sides. The beads stand for numbers. They are moved back and forth to show different amounts. The abacus is laid on a flat surface when in use.

Depending on where an abacus is made, the number of beads and the number of wires vary. The Russian abacus, for example, has ten wires with ten beads on each wire. The beads on the wire at the far right have the value of units, or ones. Those on the next wire stand for tens, those on the next wire stand for hundreds, and so on. Each time all of the beads on any one wire have been moved forward, one bead on the next wire is moved forward. The beads on the completed wire are moved back. For example, the number 149 is represented by one "hundreds" bead, four "tens" beads, and nine "ones" beads moved forward. Skilled abacus users are able to add, subtract, multiply, and divide quickly by moving the beads. *See also* COMPUTER.

J.J.A.; P.Q.F./S.P.A.; L.W.

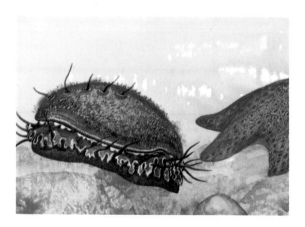

The abalone is a single-shelled mollusk. A main feature of the abalone is the row of holes in its shell.

ABALONE (ab′ə lō′nē) The abalone is a large marine mollusk belonging to the class Gastropoda. (*See* GASTROPOD.) The abalone is found off the coasts of California, Australia, and South Africa. The abalone has one shell, which is shaped like a bowl. It covers the top of the animal. The abalone grows up to 1 ft. [30 cm] long. There is a row of holes along one edge of the shell through which water passes. The gills of the abalone enable it to breathe the way fish breathe. The inside of the shell is a beautiful white mineral that is called mother-of-pearl. Mother-of-pearl is used in jewelry and other decorative items. The abalone's large, muscular foot is called abalone steak when it is eaten by humans. S.R.G./C.S.H.

ABDOMEN (ab′də mən) The abdomen is a section of the body of an animal. People often call it the belly. In humans, the abdomen begins at the bottom of the ribs and ends at the hips. The abdomen contains many important organs, such as the stomach, the intestines, the kidneys, and the liver. These organs are kept in place by strong muscles. A muscular membrane called the diaphragm separates the abdomen from the chest cavity, where the lungs and heart are. *See also* ANATOMY.

In insects, the abdomen is the last body region. No legs are attached to this part of the body. *See also* INSECT. S.R.G./M.J.C.; J.J.F.; M.H.M.

ABERRATION (ab′ə rā′shən) An aberration is a defect in an image formed by the lenses and curved mirrors of optical instruments, such as telescopes and microscopes. The aberration occurs because the light rays from an object are not brought to a sharp focus.

Two important forms of aberration are chromatic and spherical. Chromatic aberrations are the colored fringes that sometimes occur along the edge of an image produced by a lens or mirror. Chromatic aberration occurs because the lens or mirror bends blue light more than red light. A spherical aberration occurs when a lens or mirror brings light rays to focus in slightly different positions. This makes the image fuzzy. *See also* LENS; OPTICS.

P.Q.F; W.R.P./S.S.B.; L.W.

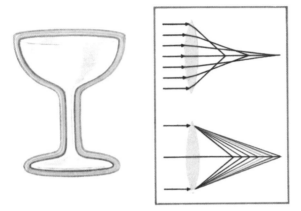

The colored sparkle of a wine glass (above left) is due to chromatic aberration. The diagram (above right) shows two kinds of aberration that are seen when light passes through a lens. The upper lens shows spherical aberration. The lower lens shows chromatic aberration.

ABORIGINE (ab'ə rij'ə nē) The Aborigines are Australia's original inhabitants. They are a dark-skinned people thought to have no close relationship to any other race living today.

Scientists think the first Aborigines migrated to Australia from Southeast Asia many thousands of years ago. Experts are not sure exactly when the Aborigines first arrived. However, it is thought that they have been in Australia for thirty thousand years or longer. It is estimated that there were 250,000 or more Aborigines living in Australia when the first white settlers arrived in the 1700s from Britain.

Over the thousands of years that the Aborigines have been in Australia, they have adapted to the harsh environments, such as desert conditions, in which they live. For example, the tribes whose territory did not

have rivers or streams dug deeply into the soil to find a few drops of moisture or shook dew off plants in the early morning. The water they found was not used for bathing, but rather for drinking only at the beginning and end of the day.

Before the first white settlers arrived in Australia, the Aborigines did not grow their own food or live in any one location for long. They were nomads, carrying few belongings and moving from place to place in search of food, water, wood for fuel, and other necessities. Each tribe, numbering about 20 to 50 people, traveled in a particular territory of several hundred square miles. Sometimes, tribes of different territories would fight over boundaries or water. The men spent much of their time hunting and fishing, using boomerangs, clubs, and spears. The women gathered plants and insects for food and medicine, using digging sticks and baskets. Aboriginal children played and learned their social roles by imitating their mothers and fathers. The children also played with the dingo, a kind of dog, which was the only domestic animal the Aborigines kept.

Religion was a very important part of Aboriginal life. Their mythical religion was based on belief in the "Eternal Dreamtime," a time long ago when humans and animals were not separate beings, but existed as unified spirits. An Aborigine believed he or she descended from a particular spirit and was linked to the animal that also descended from that spirit. This belief is called totemism. One of the ways the Aborigines expressed their beliefs was through their art, which included bark painting, body painting, dancing, and rock or cliff drawing.

The first white settlers had little or no interest in living peaceably with the Aborigines or in understanding their culture. Rather, the Aborigines were mainly looked upon as an annoyance. Shortly after the white settlers arrived, many Aborigines had been forced from their traditional territories. Many others were killed in clashes with the settlers over land and water or by the diseases the white settlers brought with them. The traditional Aboriginal way of life was almost destroyed.

Today, the Australian government is working hard to make up for the past. In 1962, the Aborigines were given full citizenship. Shortly afterward, measures were passed to end discrimination against the Aborigines. The government has established many programs to try to improve housing, health care, employment, and education for the Aborigines. Reserves have also been set up for those who wish to follow the traditional Aboriginal way of life. *See also* AUSTRALOID. P.Q.F./J.E.P.

ABORTION (ə bȯr′shən) An abortion is the death of a fetus (unborn child) during the first nineteen weeks of pregnancy. The mother's body will usually reject the dead fetus, causing it to leave her body. At other times, a doctor must remove the dead fetus. The fetus's death may be caused by many things. The fetus may develop incorrectly, or the mother may become ill or be injured. The death of a fetus is also called a miscarriage.

Sometimes the fetus is not healthy. Sometimes the mother's health is in danger. In such cases, doctors may cause the abortion of the fetus. It used to be illegal for doctors to perform an abortion unless the mother's life was in danger. Today, in many areas of the United States, doctors are allowed to perform abortions because the mother does not wish to have a baby, even if she is healthy.

S.R.G./J.J.F.; M.H.M.

ABRASIVE (ə brā′siv) An abrasive is a material used to grind, wear down, scrape, or polish other materials. The two main forms of abrasives are paper and grinding wheels. Abrasive paper is made by coating paper with a glue and adding the abrasive substance. Sandpaper, emery paper, and Carborundum paper are made in this way. To make a grinding wheel, abrasive material such as quartz is mixed with clay and water. This mixture is then pressed into the desired size and shape and fired in a furnace. The heat makes a strong bond among the materials.

A grit number is used to describe the fineness or coarseness of the particles used in an abrasive material. Abrasives with a grit number of 60 are much finer than abrasives with a grit number of 30. The hardness of an abrasive is important. An abrasive must be harder than the material it is meant to grind or polish. The hardness of minerals is measured according to a scale known as Mohs scale. (*See* HARDNESS.)

The most widely used abrasives are fused aluminum oxide (Al_2O_3) and silicon carbide (SiC). Aluminum oxide is known as alumina. It is used to grind and polish metals such as steel, wrought iron, and hard bronze. Silicon carbide is better known as Carborundum. It is made by fusing sand and coke in an electric furnace. Carborundum is used to grind and polish brass, copper, aluminum, stone, glass, and ceramics.

Varieties of quartz are also important abrasives. Pumice is a volcanic rock. When ground to a fine powder, it is used in scouring powders and soaps. Diatomite is the chalky remains of tiny organisms. (*See* DIATOM.) It is used in metal polishes. Crystalline iron oxide is used to polish jewelry and glass. It is known as jeweler's rouge because of its reddish color.

Abrasive wheels like this one are used to grind and polish many different kinds of materials.

Synthetic diamonds and diamonds not suitable for gemstones are used as abrasives. They provide a hard edge in the drill bits used in drilling through rock for oil. Tungsten carbide (WC) is used in the machine-tool industry for the drilling, cutting, and polishing of metals. The carbides, nitrides, and borides of tantalum, vanadium, and zirconium are similar in hardness to tungsten carbide and are used for the same purposes. Another important abrasive is boron carbide (B_4C). It is valuable because it is almost as hard as diamond.

J.J.A./R.H.

ABSOLUTE ZERO Absolute zero, the complete absence of heat, is a concept derived from the third law of thermodynamics, according to which the lowest temperature possible is -459.67°F. [-273.15°C]. (*See* THERMODYNAMICS.) These numbers are based on the theory that the volume of a gas gets smaller as its temperature is lowered. (*See* CHARLES'S LAW.) In this theory, the volume of a gas would disappear if its temperature were lowered to -459.67°F., or absolute zero. The gas molecules would be completely at rest, and the substance would possess no heat at all. In actual practice, however, all gases change to liquids and/or solids before their temperature reaches absolute zero.

Scientists have never been able to reach absolute zero in laboratory experiments, though they have come close. Materials cooled to temperatures near absolute zero react strangely. Oxygen freezes to a bluish white solid; a rubber ball becomes so brittle that it shatters instead of bouncing. Mercury, normally liquid, looks and acts like hard silver. Hydrogen becomes a liquid and begins creeping up the sides of its container. Natural gas is shipped in special containers after being cooled and liquefied in this way.

The temperature at which the volume of a gas would disappear is given the value of zero on the Kelvin scale. The Kelvin scale is used for scientific measurements. Absolute zero on the Kelvin scale is expressed as zero Kelvin (0 K). The degree sign (°) is not used in the Kelvin scale. *See also* CRYOGENICS; KELVIN SCALE; KELVIN, LORD.

W.R.P./R.W.L.

ABSORPTION AND ADSORPTION

Absorption (əb sȯrp′shən) and adsorption (ad sȯrp′shən) are two different ways for a substance to take up another substance. In absorption, the second substance becomes spread throughout the first substance. In adsorption, the second substance is spread only on the surface of the first substance.

Substances can also absorb various forms of energy, such as heat, light, and sound. When energy is absorbed by an object, the energy usually changes form. For example, people are warmed, and their skin may become reddened or darker, when they absorb the sun's rays. All colored objects have a certain color because they reflect that color. They absorb all the others. For example, a blue object absorbs nearly all the light striking its surface except blue light, which is reflected. Sunlight and other white light are a mixture of all colors. A black object absorbs all of the light falling on it. Sound is absorbed by heavy curtains and soundproofing materials. These materials are often found in recording studios, concert halls, and auditoriums. The materials absorb internally produced sounds and prevent them from producing echoes and reverberations.

Liquids absorb solids and gases by dissolving them. The sea absorbs oxygen from the air and from plant life in the water. The absorption of gases is important in industry. Many gases are purified by passing them up a tower containing streams of falling liquid. The liquid absorbs the impurities in the gases. The towers are called absorption towers or scrubbers.

In the body, nutrients from food are absorbed after digestion through the wall of the gastrointestinal tract. Blood also absorbs oxygen from the air in the lungs and carries it to the body tissues.

When a porous solid, such as a sponge or dry earth, absorbs a liquid, what actually happens is that the countless interior surfaces of the tiny pore spaces in the solid adsorb the liquid. Solids adsorb liquids by surface attraction.

ABSORPTION AND ADSORPTION

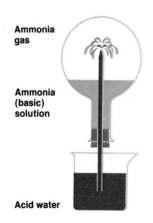

Ammonia gas

Ammonia (basic) solution

Acid water

The "ammonia fountain" (left) shows chemical absorption. Acid water is drawn up through ammonia gas and is changed to a basic solution. Litmus dye shows the changing of acid (red) to base (blue). The coloring matter (right) of brown sugar is chemically adsorbed by charcoal. When a solution of brown sugar is filtered through charcoal, it loses its brown color. The brown pigments remain in the charcoal filter. The colorless liquid is a sugar solution. Crystals of white sugar are recovered from this solution.

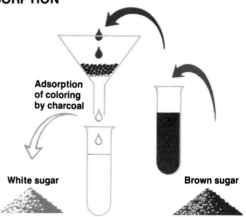

Adsorption of coloring by charcoal

White sugar

Brown sugar

In the photo at left, the earth, a solid, is absorbing rainwater, a liquid.

Solids also adsorb gases. Powerful solid adsorbents, such as charcoal, can adsorb up to ninety times their volume of a gas. Charcoal is used in gas masks to remove large amounts of poisonous or impure gases from the air that the person wearing the mask breathes. Charcoal is also used to remove odors and coloring matter from solids and liquids.

W.R.P./M.J.C.; A.D.; L.O.S.

ABYSSAL ZONE The abyssal (ə bis′əl) zone is the deepest part of the ocean and includes over 75 percent of it. The abyssal zone begins at the point at which sunlight does not penetrate. That point is about 9,843 ft. [3,000 m] below the surface of the ocean. The abyssal zone ends at the ocean floor, or bottom.

The ocean floor is covered with sediment and with microscopic and decaying organisms. Because of the lack of light, there are no green plants on the ocean floor. The floor of the ocean ranges from flatlands to hills and ridges. Ridges, which often include inactive volcanoes, can extend from the ocean floor to the surface. The tops of the ridges may be visible as islands.

The abyssal zone is very cold. The cold temperature is caused by the lack of sunlight and the sinking of cold water near the north and south poles. The cold water then spreads along the ocean floor toward the equator.

The organisms found in the abyssal zone include cephalopods, crustaceans, diatoms, fish, sea cucumbers, and snails. (*See* CEPHALOPOD; CRUSTACEAN; DIATOM; FISH; SEA CUCUMBER; SNAIL.) The organisms that live in the abyssal zone have adapted to an environment without light and to intense pressure from the water above. For example, some of the fish are blind. They use tentacles, or feelers, rather than eyes to help them find their way around. These tentacles also help them catch prey by detecting slight vibrations of moving organisms. Other organisms, such as certain cephalopods and crustaceans, have bioluminescent organs, which are organs that give off light. These organs help them attract mates or, sometimes, prey. A major food source for animals in the abyssal zone is dead plants and animals that fall from the higher depths of the ocean. *See also* OCEANOGRAPHY.   P.W./J.E.P.

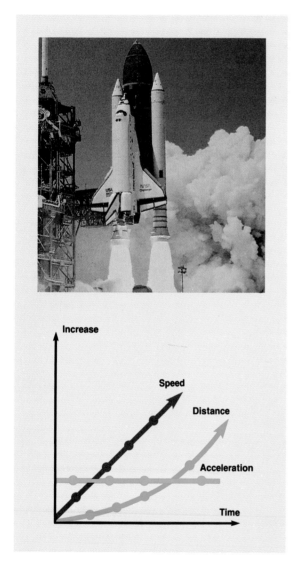

A rocket (top) will accelerate to high speed in a short time and may cover a great distance. The graph (bottom) shows how these quantities are related. Amount of increase is shown by the black arrow pointing upward, and amount of time is shown by the black arrow pointing to the side. Acceleration is the unchanging blue line. Speed is the straight red line that steadily increases. Distance is the curved green line that increases at an ever-greater rate.

ACCELERATION (ak sel′ə rā′shən) Acceleration is the rate at which the velocity of something changes. (*See* VELOCITY.) An airplane roaring down the runway during takeoff is accelerating rapidly. In a drag race, the drivers try to reach the highest possible velocity after a short distance. To do this, they have to accelerate as much as possible.

Acceleration is always caused by a force. In a car or plane, the force is produced by the engine. The amount of acceleration for a body of a certain mass is directly related to the force. If the force is doubled, the acceleration is also doubled. However, if the body is twice as heavy, the same force accelerates it only half as much. This is why a truck needs a more powerful engine than a small car.

A force can also slow an object down. The force does this when it acts in the opposite direction to the motion. This is sometimes called deceleration, but it is still acceleration.

A force can also act at an angle to the object. This changes the direction in which the object is going. This is still an acceleration because the velocity has changed. Because velocity is a speed in a particular direction, if either the speed or the direction changes, then the velocity also changes. When an object moves in a circle, its speed can stay the same but its direction is continually changing. Therefore, its velocity is continually changing. For example, the velocity of a spacecraft in orbit is always changing, even when its speed stays the same. The force that causes the velocity to change is the force of gravity. *See also* DYNAMICS.

M.E./J.T.

ACCELERATORS, PARTICLE Particle accelerators (pärt′i kəl ak sel′ə rā′tərz) are machines used by nuclear scientists to speed up the flow of subatomic particles. (*See* ATOM.) These high-speed particles are then sent smashing into a target consisting of a small amount of an element. (*See* ELEMENT.) This process is called bombardment. The high-speed particles can also be smashed into each other. This process is called collision. Depending on the process, new subatomic particles or elements may be formed. Particle accelerators are usually very large. Stanford Linear Accelerator Center (SLAC) at Stanford University in California has a linear accelerator with a tube that is 2 mi. [3.2 km] long. A linear accelerator runs in a long, straight line. The European Organization for Nuclear Research (CERN) near Geneva, Switzerland, has a circular accelerator that is 1.4 mi. [2.2 km] in diameter. Fermi National Accelerator Laboratory (Fermilab) near Batavia, Illinois, is another circular accelerator. Fermilab has a diameter of 1.25 mi. [2 km].

There are three main types of accelerators: electrostatic, linear, and circular. The electrostatic accelerator (also called a Van de Graff generator) uses very high voltage and gives only a single impulse, or push, to each particle. Linear accelerators use electromagnetic fields to give particles one boost after another as they move through long straight pipes called drift tubes. (*See* ELECTROMAGNETISM.) Circular accelerators, including cyclotrons and synchrotrons, use powerful superconducting magnets to bend the speeding particles into a circular path. (*See* SUPERCONDUCTIVITY.) Successive jolts of electricity make them go faster and faster. The energy acquired by the speeding particles in these machines can amount to more than 1 trillion electron volts. The accelerators may use as much electricity as an entire town.

Lord Ernest Rutherford, a British physicist, developed the first artificial nuclear reaction in 1919. (*See* RUTHERFORD, ERNEST.) He bombarded nitrogen nuclei with naturally produced alpha particles. (*See* ALPHA PARTICLE.) However, naturally produced particles do not have enough speed to be able to cause nuclear reactions with most nuclei. Rutherford could go no further with the experiment. Then, in 1931, Dr. Ernest Orlando Lawrence, of the University of California, invented the cyclotron. The cyclotron was a circular accelerator that greatly speeded up the motion of particles. It made a new range of experiments possible. A year later, in 1932, John Cockroft and Ernest Walton, two British physicists, built the first linear accelerator. Using the new linear accelerator, the two scientists were able, for the first time in history, to accelerate particles to speeds that would allow them to split the nucleus of an atom, a process called fission. (*See* FISSION.) Cockcroft and Walton bombarded the element lithium with a beam of protons, splitting the lithium nucleus into two halves. The nuclear fragments created in this way were themselves the nuclei of helium atoms.

Protons, electrons, and the nuclei of the lighter elements are the particles most often accelerated. For example, they can be aimed at a target, which is a nucleus of another element. When the target nucleus absorbs the bombarding particles, a different element is formed. This is called transmutation. (*See* TRANSMUTATION OF ELEMENTS.) Scientists have produced several new artificial elements this way. Some of them are neptunium, fermium, berkelium, and mendelevium. Experimenters have even been able to turn lead into gold. However, the change from lead into gold is much too costly for practical use.

Many other exciting discoveries have been made in accelerator experiments. Scientists have been able to prove the existence of many

Particle accelerators such as these at Stanford Linear Accelerator Center at Stanford University in Menlo Park, California, (top) and Fermilab near Chicago, Illinois, (bottom) are used by scientists to split atoms apart or to join atoms together.

subatomic particles that were only thought to exist. Mesons are an example of a subatomic particle that scientists have created in particle accelerators. (*See* MESON.) Mesons are lighter than protons but heavier than electrons. Mesons exist in cosmic rays. (*See* COSMIC RAYS.) However, they are short-lived, so they are difficult to observe. The neutrino is another particle that scientists have been able to create and study in particle accelerators. The neutrino is abundant in nature and has a very small mass—probably none at all when at rest. (*See* NEUTRINO.)

The study of how particles react when bombarded or collided is called particle physics or high energy physics. (*See* PARTICLE PHYSICS.) A high energy physics center with a particle accelerator is a large place containing some of the most complicated and expensive equipment in the world. The hundreds of scientists and technicians who work there are carefully protected from the dangerous particle beams and the intense electrical voltages.

Thousands of reactions from bombardments and collisions must be analyzed before scientists can be sure of the results. Three kinds of detectors, or chambers, are used in this work. One kind of chamber is a bubble chamber, which is a tank containing a liquid that is near its boiling point. Particles from a reaction, made to travel through this liquid, leave behind a visible trail of bubbles. Another kind of chamber is a cloud chamber, which directs particles through a cloud of cooled gases. This causes the particles to leave visible condensation trails. A final kind of chamber used for bombardments and collisions is a spark chamber. In a spark chamber, particles leave a trail of sparks as they pass through electrified metal plates. The trails in all three kinds of chambers are photographed auto-

matically and analyzed by computers. *See also* ELECTRON; IONS AND IONIZATION; NEUTRON; NUCLEUS, ATOMIC; PROTON.

C.C.; W.R.P./E.W.L.; J.T.

ACCOMMODATION (ə käm′ə dā′shən) The automatic adjustment of the eyes that allows them to focus on an object is called accommodation. Each eye has a lens near its front that bends incoming light rays to focus on the light-sensitive lining of the eyeball, called the retina. The retina is connected to the brain by a nerve. The lens is flexible, and its thickness

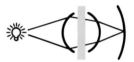

When a person looks at an object, the eye often must accommodate so that the object can be seen clearly. The light from a nearby object must be bent by the lens of each eye in order to focus the light on the retina. The lens accommodates by becoming thicker. The diagram above shows this.

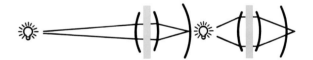

Light from a faraway object needs less bending to focus on the retina of the eye. In this case, most of the bending, or refraction, of the light occurs in the cornea of the eye. There is no accommodation of the lens. The diagram above left shows this. As a person ages, the lenses of the eyes accommodate less easily. Light from nearby objects comes to a focus behind the retina. This gives the person blurred vision called farsightedness, and glasses are needed for close work, such as reading. The diagram above right shows this.

can be changed by muscles called ciliary muscles. During accommodation, the ciliary muscles make the lens thicker or thinner so that light rays from the object being looked at are clearly focused on the retina.

S.R.G./S.S.B.; M.H.M.

ACETAMINOPHEN *See* ANALGESIC; ASPIRIN.

ACETATE *See* ACETIC ACID.

ACETIC ACID (ə sēt′ik as′əd) Acetic acid is an organic acid with a strong, vinegarlike smell. Acetic acid is formed in the fermentation process sometimes used for making vinegar. Vinegar contains about 5 percent acetic acid. However, vinegar is most often produced by the use of chemicals. Acetic acid is used to make acetates. Acetates are the substances that acetic acid forms with bases or alcohols. (*See* ALCOHOL; BASE.) The most important acetates are cellulose acetate and vinyl acetate. They are both used in plastics. (*See* CELLULOSE ACETATE.) Acetic acid is also used as a chemical solvent, as a food preservative, and in photographic processing.

Acetic acid's chemical formula is CH_3COOH. Pure acetic acid is a colorless liquid that corrodes other objects. The boiling point of acetic acid is 244°F. [118°C]. Its freezing point is 62°F. [17°C]. In a cool atmosphere, the pure acid turns solid, forming white, icy crystals. The pure form is known as glacial acetic acid.   J.J.A./J.M.

ACETONE (as′ə tōn′) Acetone is a colorless liquid with a sweet odor. Acetone dissolves many substances. It is used as a solvent in industry. Acetone is also used in the making of acetate rayon, thread, photographic film, and fingernail polish.

Acetone's chemical formula is CH_3COCH_3. It is also called dimethyl ketone. Acetone has a boiling point of 133.7°F. [56.5°C]. Its freezing point is -139°F. [-95°C]. Acetone can be obtained from the distillation of wood or from the bacterial fermentation of molasses. It can also be made by other chemical methods. *See also* DISTILLATION; FERMENTATION.   J.J.A./J.M.

ACETYLENE (ə set′l ēn) Acetylene is a colorless, poisonous gas, with a chemical formula of C_2H_2. Acetylene is made from calcium carbide and water. Because it burns easily, the main use of acetylene is in the

A worker uses an oxyacetylene torch. The torch provides enough heat to enable it to cut through metal.

welding and cutting of metals with an oxyacetylene torch. (*See* OXYACETYLENE TORCH.) When acetylene burns, it reaches a temperature of 6,332°F. [3,500°C] or more. At this high temperature, it can cut metal that is several inches thick. Chemists often call acetylene *ethyne.*

Acetylene dissolves easily in acetone. It does not dissolve as well in water or alcohol. It dissolves more easily at low temperatures and under high pressure. Acetylene cannot be compressed without danger of explosion. It is stored and transported in cylinders containing acetone.

Substances made from acetylene include vinyl plastics, synthetic rubber and fibers, and many organic chemicals. Acetylene was once commonly used for light in portable lamps, buoys, and road signals. J.J.A./J.M.

ACHERNAR *See* STAR.

ACHILLES TENDON The Achilles (ə kil′ēz) tendon is located on the lower leg of humans. It connects the gastrocnemius muscle, which

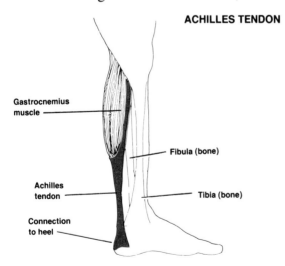

ACHILLES TENDON

Gastrocnemius muscle

Fibula (bone)

Achilles tendon

Tibia (bone)

Connection to heel

The Achilles tendon connects the large calf muscle of the leg, called the gastrocnemius, to the heel bone of the foot.

is the large calf muscle of the leg, to the heel bone of the foot. (*See* GASTROCNEMIUS; TENDON.) The Achilles is the largest tendon in the human body. The gastrocnemius muscle and the Achilles tendon pull the heel bone up, making it possible for a person to walk, run, or stand on the toes.

The Achilles tendon gets its name from Greek mythology. It was said that the Greek hero Achilles could not be harmed or wounded anywhere on his body, except for the heel of his foot. That is where the Achilles tendon connects to the bone. S.R.G./J.J.F.; M.H.M.

ACID (as′əd) Acids are a group of chemicals with certain similar characteristics. For example, all acids have a sour taste. The citric acid in lemon juice makes it taste sour. Vinegar tastes sour because it contains acetic acid. The acids in lemon juice and vinegar are diluted with water. They cause no harm to the body. However, other acids can be dangerous. For example, hydrofluoric acid is so powerful it can corrode and dissolve metals and glass. A substance that can corrode is also called caustic. (*See* CORROSION.)

Life depends on acid. For example, human stomachs contain diluted hydrochloric acid, which helps digest food. (*See* HYDROCHLORIC ACID.) Amino acids are also essential. Human beings need eight special amino acids to stay alive. (*See* AMINO ACID.) Ascorbic acid from fruits and vegetables is important as well. Ascorbic acid is vitamin C. If a person does not eat foods that contain vitamin C, he or she will become sick with the disease called scurvy. (*See* SCURVY.)

Acids are important in industry. For example, millions of tons of sulfuric acid are made every year. Sulfuric acid is used to dissolve the rust and scale on iron. (*See* SULFURIC

ACID.) This type of cleaning is called pickling. Acids are also used in making fertilizers, pigments and dyes, plastics, and synthetic fibers. Aqua regia is a mixture of nitric and hydrochloric acids. (*See* NITRIC ACID.) Aqua regia is used to dissolve gold and platinum.

There are two main chemical groups of acids. They are inorganic acids and organic acids. Organic acids contain carbon; inorganic acids do not. The one thing all acids have in common is that when they dissolve in water, they release hydrogen ions (H^+). Hydrogen ions are hydrogen atoms with a positive electric charge. (*See* IONS AND IONIZATION.) Acids that make a large number of hydrogen ions in water are strong acids. Hydrochloric acid, nitric acid, and sulfuric acid are examples of strong acids. With the strongest acids, such as hydrochloric acid, all the molecules split up to give hydrogen ions. Acids that make few hydrogen ions in water are weak acids. Acetic acid, citric acid, and carbonic acid are examples of weak acids.

Chemists can measure the strength of hydrogen ions in a solution. This is called the pH of a solution. Acids have a pH of 0 to 7. Acids with a low pH number, such as 2, are stronger than acids with a high pH number, such as 6.

One way to tell whether or not a substance is an acid is to use an indicator. An indicator is an object that turns a certain color in an acid. Litmus paper is an indicator that turns from blue to red in an acid. No one should ever taste unknown solutions to find out whether or not they are acids. Certain acids burn or wound the tongue and skin. Other acids are poisonous.

Many foods turn sour when they spoil. Their starches and sugars break down into acids. For example, when milk turns sour, some of the milk sugar is changed to lactic acid. Butter that spoils contains butyric acid.

If certain metals, such as iron or zinc, are added to acid solutions, the metal dissolves. Hydrogen gas (H_2) is also produced from this reaction. This happens because the atoms from the metal and the hydrogen ions from the acid combine. Together, they make hydrogen gas and metal ions. The metal ions combine with the acid to produce a salt. In this way, the metal replaces the hydrogen in the acid. For example, if zinc (Zn) is added to hydrochloric acid (HCl), zinc chloride ($ZnCl_2$), a salt, and hydrogen gas (H_2) are produced. *See also* BASE; NEUTRALIZATION.

J.J.A./A.D.; E.D.W.

ACID PRECIPITATION *See* ACID RAIN.

PROJECT

ACID RAIN Acid (as′əd) rain is pollution that falls to the earth as rain that is more acidic than natural rain. Scientists also include other forms of acidic precipitation, such as mist, hail, sleet, and snow, in the term *acid rain*. Acid rain is a serious problem all over the world. It weakens and kills many organisms. In some places, acid rain has permanently damaged trees, flowers, and other plants by changing their metabolisms. For example, trees affected by acid rain may not be able to prepare properly for cold weather. Acid rain has also caused many streams, lakes, and other bodies of water to become too acidic for fish and other organisms to live and reproduce in them. In some places, the rain is so acidic that it eats away at human-made objects such as buildings, statues, and the paint on cars.

Acid rain forms when water and certain gases in the atmosphere mix. These gases contain sulfur and nitrogen. This mixture produces sulfuric and nitric acid. These acids

Acid rain has been shown to harm many different kinds of plants. These dead and dying needles are on an evergreen in the eastern United States that has been damaged by acid rain.

later fall to the ground in acid rain. Some of the sulfur and nitrogen in the atmosphere come from natural sources. These include forest fires, volcanic eruptions, and lightning. However, human activities—such as burning coal and oil in factories and power plants and burning fuel in cars and trucks—also produce huge amounts of sulfur and nitrogen. Many scientists feel that these human activities produce most of the acid rain that falls.

Scientists call acid rain a long-range pollutant. The sulfur and nitrogen needed to make acid rain can travel long distances in the atmosphere. Acid rain can then fall hundreds of miles from the sources of nitrogen and sulfur that produced it. Thus, the fish in a stream in Vermont or the trees in a forest in Massachusetts may be harmed by acid rain caused by sulfur from a smokestack in Ohio or Pennsylvania.

Keeping the atmosphere clean from sulfur and nitrogen pollutants is the only answer to the problem. There is no effective, cost-efficient way to completely remove all the sulfur and nitrogen from the smoke and exhaust fumes that factories, power plants, and vehicles give off. However, steps are being taken by some coal-burning electric-power plants to reduce the amount of harmful chemicals the plants release into the atmosphere. Many electric-power plants in the United States burn coal that contains large amounts of sulfur. Much of this sulfur enters the atmosphere in the smoke that these plants release. Changing to low-sulfur coal, which is more expensive, helps reduce the amount of sulfur released. Electric-power companies are also installing "scrubbers," or filters, to remove sulfur from the smoke that their plants release.

Fortunately, it is sometimes possible to undo the harm from acid rain. Scientists are starting to treat bodies of water harmed by acid rain with lime. The lime neutralizes the acid in the water, and, in many cases, fish and other organisms can live in it once more. However, the water may never return to the condition it was before being polluted. *See also* ACID; NITROGEN; POLLUTION; SULFUR.

P.Q.F./J.E.P.

ACNE (ak'nē) Acne is a disorder of the sebaceous glands of the skin. Sebaceous glands normally secrete a fatty substance called sebum. If allowed to accumulate, sebum becomes mixed with dust and dirt, causing inflammation and the eruption of pimples. Because acne is related to hormonal changes that occur during adolescence, teenagers often have acne. Cleanliness and diet also affect the condition of a person's skin. To treat acne, doctors recommend keeping one's skin clean and not eating a lot of sweets. Serious cases of acne are treated with prescription drugs. Doctors who specialize in treatment of acne and other skin disorders are called dermatologists. *See also* SKIN.   S.R.G./J.J.F.

ACOUSTICS (ə kü'stiks) Acoustics is the branch of the science and technology of sound that deals with how to use and control sound waves. An important part of acoustics is the study of architectural acoustics, or how sound behaves in a room or building.

Architectural acoustics The aim of architectural acoustics is to design rooms with good sound qualities. This is very important in buildings such as concert halls and theaters. In these buildings, the sound should be neither too loud nor too soft. People expect to be able to hear clearly wherever they are sitting.

In a room, some materials, such as plaster, reflect sound. Other materials, such as carpets, absorb sound. In an auditorium, there has to be just the right balance and placement of materials. This ensures that the sound is evenly spread.

Sound has two properties that are very important in acoustics. These properties are echo and reverberation. An echo is a sound that has been reflected (thrown back) from a

Scientists use "quiet rooms," such as this one at Bell Laboratories in New Jersey, to study how sound behaves.

surface. Materials that reflect sound well produce strong echoes. In an auditorium, people hear the sound both directly from the stage and from the echo. Because the echo has bounced off a surface, it has traveled farther than the direct sound. This means that it reaches the ear after the direct sound does. In a well-designed room, the echo and the direct sound are heard almost at the same time. The sound is then clearly heard. (*See* ECHO.)

A reverberation is a closely grouped series of echoes. Each echo is quieter than the one before. Rooms could be built with sound-absorbent materials to remove reverberations and echoes. However, the sound in such a room would have a dead quality. A certain amount of reverberation is necessary for good sound quality. In general, the reverberations should last between 1 and 2.5 seconds. This is called the reverberation time. It is the time taken for all echoes to die away. Rooms used for music should have a slightly longer reverberation time than rooms used for speech.

Another problem in designing an auditorium is the volume of sound. People sitting at the back should be able to hear clearly. Sometimes, this means that the sound has to be amplified by loudspeakers. Unfortunately, loudspeakers rarely reproduce the sound accurately. (*See* LOUDSPEAKER.)

The pitch, or frequency, of a sound must also be considered. Sounds with different pitch can be reflected from surfaces in different amounts. Resonance must also be avoided. (*See* FREQUENCY; RESONANCE.) Both these effects cause either the high or the low frequencies to sound too loud. If the high frequencies are too loud, the sound has a shrill, thin quality. If the low frequencies are too loud, the sound is dull and muffled.

The ancient Greeks were the first to build their theaters acoustically. They placed their audiences on steep hillsides where sound could travel to them directly. Their theaters were called amphitheaters. The stage was at the bottom of rows of seating that were steeply inclined. Every member of the audience could see and hear well. This idea was copied by the Romans. The Hollywood Bowl, in California, is a modern-day amphitheater.

Other branches of acoustics Although architectural acoustics is an important field, acoustics has other, very different branches.

In communications acoustics, engineers are trying to build machines that can speak and hear. This is a very difficult task. Human speech is a complicated mixture of frequencies. The brain can easily put all these different frequencies together so that a spoken word is heard. Machines cannot do this yet, but progress is being made. Such machines would be very useful in banks. In a bank, the identity of a customer is checked by his or her signature. It is very difficult for anybody to copy another person's signature. However, it

At the Hollywood Bowl, a modern amphitheater, all members of the audience can hear well.

is not impossible. A better method of checking a person's identity would be from the pattern of his or her speech. This pattern is unique and impossible to copy.

Machines that can speak and hear can also be useful in the field of computers. A number of computer functions can now be activated by human speech. In addition, computers have the ability to talk to people through voice synthesizers. Today, for example, many automatic banking machines, automobiles, videocassette recorders, and other appliances have voice synthesizers. A synthesized voice may give the correct telephone numbers to people who dial directory assistance.

Ultrasonics is another important branch of acoustics. Ultrasonics is the study of sound waves that have too high a frequency to be heard. Normally, a sound wave travels smoothly through an object. However, if the object has a crack in it, the waves are reflected and refracted (bent). Ultrasonics is used to detect cracks in such objects as engine parts or spacecraft components. Ultrasonic waves, rather than sound waves, are used because they are refracted at a larger angle. This makes the cracks more easily detectable. *See also* SOUND; ULTRASOUND.   M.E./R.W.L.

ACRYLIC (ə kril'ik) An acrylic is any of a group of synthetic (human-made) products made mostly from petroleum. Acrylics are manufactured as fibers, plastics, or resins. (*See* FIBER; PLASTIC; RESIN.)

Acrylic fibers are made into many kinds of fabrics. These fabrics are used in blankets, carpets, underwear, and knitwear. Common trade names for some acrylic fibers are Acrilan, Creslan, Zefran, and Orlon.

A widely used acrylic plastic is polymethyl methacrylate. Plastics made from this

In this factory, acrylic fibers are being baled before being spun into thread for fabrics.

substance are better known as Plexiglas and Lucite. They are important because they are transparent. They are used to make windows, television lenses, outdoor signs, automobile taillights, dishes, surgical tools, and costume jewelry.

Although acrylics stand up well under bad weather conditions, they are softer than glass. Therefore, they scratch easily.   J.J.A./J.M.

ACTH *See* ADRENAL GLANDS.

ACTINIUM *See* ELEMENT.

ACUPUNCTURE (ak'yü pungk'chər) Acupuncture is an ancient Chinese technique for relieving pain for such conditions as arthritis, asthma, migraine headaches, and ulcers. The technique involves inserting long, thin needles into specific points on the body. There are about one thousand acupuncture points, each identified by name and number. Each point belongs to one of fourteen groups associated with a particular internal body organ.

Treatment involves inserting a number of needles at various angles and depths. The needles are twisted or vibrated to provide stimulation. This stimulation may provide permanent or temporary relief, depending on the condition.

Traditional Chinese theories state that acupuncture relieves pain because it restores harmony in the body. One modern scientific theory suggests that acupuncture works by triggering the release of pain-relieving substances called endorphins. (*See* ENDORPHIN.) Another theory says that acupuncture stimulates certain nerves to carry non-pain impulses. These scientific theories have made acupuncture more widely accepted around the world. Acupuncture is now sometimes used as an alternative to drugs and anesthetics in the United States and other Western countries. (*See* ANESTHETIC.) Because acupuncture carries a slight risk of infection or damage to nerves and blood vessels, some states require acupuncturists (those who perform acupuncture) to be medical doctors.

P.W./J.E.P.

ADAMS, JOHN COUCH *See* NEPTUNE.

ADAPTATION (ad'ap'tā'shən) Adaptation is a process in which living things change with new environmental conditions. There are two kinds of adaptation. One is the kind that occurs in an individual organism during its lifetime. The other kind occurs, through evolution, in a group of organisms over thousands or millions of years. (*See* EVOLUTION.)

If a person begins a new nighttime job—after working during the day all of his or her life—he or she must adapt to a new way of life. At first, the person may have difficulty sleeping during the day. After a while, however, he or she sleeps easily. The person has

The beaks of birds are adapted for particular ways of feeding. Birds that live on or near water, such as the flamingo, have plant-scooping mouth parts. The crossbill digs seeds out of pinecones with ease due to the shape of its beak. The inside of the goose's beak is very sensitive, helping the bird find food by touch. The kingfisher and woodpecker have spears that stab their prey. The long beak of the hummingbird is specialized for nectar sipping.

ADAPTATION

flamingo

crossbill

white-fronted goose

common kingfisher

great spotted woodpecker

pufflegs hummingbird

Examples of adaptation: The giraffe's long neck (above left) allows it to eat leaves that most other grazing animals cannot reach. The prickly pear cactus (top right) stores precious water in its stem. The long legs and sharp beak of a wading bird (bottom right) help it in its hunt for fish.

adapted. This is an example of individual adaptation.

The giraffe provides an example of how a group adapts to changing conditions by evolving as individual members. Thousands of years ago, giraffes, like horses, had short necks and ate grass. During a long dry period, much of the grass in Africa died. Some giraffes, the ones with the longest necks, adapted by eating the leaves of trees. They survived and reproduced. Their offspring had long necks also. As time went on, the trees grew higher, and giraffes had to reach higher to eat the leaves. In this way, long-necked giraffes always had an advantage. The result was that giraffes today have much longer necks than giraffes had thousands of years ago.

Some living things are able to adapt easily, while others cannot. Perhaps dinosaurs became extinct because they could not adapt to sudden or rapid changes in the climate of the earth. Humans are very adaptable. With special equipment, we can live anywhere on earth. We can even visit the moon.

S.R.G./R.J.B.

ADDER (ad′ər) Adder is the name for several species of snakes. Some are poisonous, and some are not. There are many species of adders found in Europe, Asia, and Africa. Adders grow from 1 ft. [0.3 m] to 6 ft. [1.8 m] in length. Their colors vary with species and geographical location. Poisonous adders kill their prey by biting. The snake injects venom, a poisonous substance, with its two long fangs. After the bitten animal dies, the adder swallows it whole. An adder can kill as soon as it is born or hatches from its egg. Adders found in the colder regions of Europe and Asia spend the winters in hibernation. (*See* HIBERNATION.)

One of the best-known adders is the European viper. Like most adders, it belongs to the viper family. (*See* VIPER.) It lives in Europe and Asia as far north as the arctic circle. It hunts at night for rodents, birds, lizards, and amphibians. The European viper grows to a length of 2 ft. [0.6 m]. Its bite can be fatal to humans. The puff adder of Africa is one of the largest, growing to a length of 4.5 ft. [1.35 m]. The puff adder is as thick as a person's arm and also has a poisonous bite.

S.R.G./C.J.C.

The adder known as the European viper is about 2 ft. (0.6 m) long. It is easily recognized by its zigzag pattern. Like other vipers, this snake has poison fangs set on a movable bone at the front of its upper jaw.

ADDICTION (ə dik′shən) Addiction is a harmful psychological and physical dependence that can result from regular use of certain drugs, such as alcohol, amphetamines, and heroin and other narcotics. Although a person may become psychologically dependent on the caffeine in coffee or the nicotine in cigarettes, such habits can be broken. With development of addiction, changes in the body's chemistry produce unpleasant, even painful, symptoms when the drug is withheld. In addition, drug addiction is often the cause of serious medical problems such as liver damage. Social complications also are common with addiction. When a person is addicted to a drug, he or she may have problems with family, friends, work, or school. Also, the illegal trade in drugs gives rise to many other crimes. *See also* DRUG.   P.Q.F./M.H.M.

ADENOID (ad′noid) The adenoids are a mass of tissue found at the back of the nasal passages leading to the throat. The adenoids, a kind of tonsil, help protect the body against infection. However, the adenoids themselves often become infected and swollen. This causes a sore throat and may make breathing difficult. It may also lead to loss of hearing. Thus, when adenoids become infected, a surgeon will often remove them. A person can stay healthy without adenoids. *See also* LYMPHATIC SYSTEM; TONSIL.   S.R.G./J.J.F.; M.H.M.

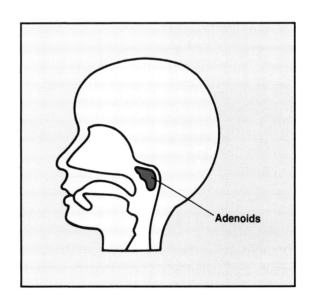

The normal function of adenoids is to protect against infection. When infected, adenoids can be removed.

ADHESION (ad hē′zhən) Adhesion is the electrical attraction of molecules of one substance to those of a different substance. The substances will stick together. If you put your finger in a glass of water, some of the water will cling to your finger after you withdraw it. That is adhesion. However, if a person puts a well-greased finger into a glass of water, no water will cling to the finger when he or she removes it. That is because the force of attraction between the molecules of water is greater than the force of adhesion between the molecules of water and the grease on the skin. The attraction of molecules to other molecules of the same substance is called cohesion. *See also* COHESION; MOLECULE; SURFACE TENSION.

S.R.G./A.D.

ADHESIVE (ad hē′siv) Adhesives are substances that stick to other substances. They make it possible for materials to be joined together. There are three main types of adhesives: structural, holding, and sealing.

A good example of a structural adhesive is the cement used for making model airplanes. Waterproof glues used in boat building are another example. Holding adhesives include library paste, mucilage, and cellophane tape. They are used to stick paper together or fasten light objects to walls. Sealing adhesives are used to stop leaks in boats or between bathroom tiles.

Adhesives used to be made from animal and plant sources. Early glues were made by boiling fish heads and bones. Others were made from gums, like gum arabic, that come from trees. Today, most household glues are made from chemicals. Of these chemical glues, plastic adhesives make up the largest groups. The epoxy resin types are among the strongest and most useful. The epoxies allow

Water in a glass tube (top left) adheres, or clings, to the walls of the tube, forming a meniscus, or curved surface, that is concave. The water molecules are attracted to the molecules of the glass. However, the molecules of mercury (bottom left) attract one another more than they are attracted to the glass of a tube. This causes a convex meniscus.

The special household glues called instant glues are so strong that a single drop can hold thousands of pounds of weight.

wood, metal, glass, concrete, and ceramics to be joined together. The joints are very strong, usually much stronger than the materials being joined. Epoxies are made in two parts: the base and the catalyst. A chemical reaction occurs when the two are mixed together. The glue must be used quickly or it will harden and become useless. (*See* EPOXY RESIN.)

Rubber serves as the base for a group of adhesives. This group is used for joining leather, rubber, textiles, plastics, and paper. Rubber-based glues and cements are used when the object to be glued will be around water. For example, rubber-based adhesives are used to stick plastic tiles to cement floors in kitchens and bathrooms. Adhesives without a rubber base would not hold down the tiles if water were spilled.

Special household glues have been developed. They are called instant glues and require no mixing. They are so strong that a single drop can hold thousands of pounds of weight. Portland cement is another kind of adhesive. It hardens to form a bond between sand and stones to make concrete. *See also* ADHESION; CEMENT AND CONCRETE. W.R.P./A.D.

ADOLESCENCE (ad′l es′ns) Adolescence is a time of growth and change that begins with sexual maturing, called puberty. (*See* PUBERTY.) Growth during adolescence, which usually occurs between the ages of twelve and twenty, depends on increased activity by the adrenal, pituitary, and sex glands. (*See* ADRENAL GLANDS; ENDOCRINE; HORMONE.) This increased activity causes physical changes to occur in adolescents. For example, menstruation begins in adolescent girls, and hair begins growing on the faces of adolescent boys. (*See* MENSTRUAL CYCLE.) These physical changes happen at different rates among adolescents. Most young people can reproduce by age fourteen or fifteen. (*See* REPRODUCTION.)

Adolescence is also a time for social growth. Adolescents develop socially by learning to act independently and by accepting responsibility for their actions. All adolescents face problems from time to time. Most problems center on school, handling money, and relationships with family and friends.

P.W./J.E.P.

ADRENAL GLANDS The adrenal (ə drē′nl) glands are small glands located above the kidneys. They are part of the endocrine system, a group of glands in the body that produces chemicals called hormones. Hormones are released into the bloodstream to control many of the body's functions. Each hormone controls a different function. (*See* ENDOCRINE; HORMONE.)

Lions chase a zebra in the wild. The animals pictured are experiencing the effects of adrenaline. Adrenaline is a hormone that gives animals, including people, extra energy in times of stress, such as during a chase.

The adrenal glands have two parts: the adrenal cortex on the outside and the adrenal medulla on the inside. The adrenal cortex produces many hormones. Some regulate the way the body uses sugar. Other hormones from the adrenal cortex keep the amount of salt in the blood at the right level. If the adrenal cortex does not produce enough hormones, serious illness or even death may result.

The adrenal cortex produces its hormones when another hormone, adrenocorticotropic hormone, known by its initials ACTH, enters the adrenal glands from the bloodstream. ACTH is produced in the pituitary gland, which is located at the base of the brain. The best known hormone of the adrenal cortex is cortisol.

When the adrenal medulla receives a certain signal from the brain, it produces a hormone called adrenaline. Adrenaline gives the body extra energy in times of stress. Someone who has been frightened is able to run faster and longer than usual partly because of the adrenaline released into the bloodstream by the adrenal medulla. When a person is frightened, but does not run, his or her hands may shake due to the adrenaline in the blood.

S.R.G./J.J.F.; M.H.M.

ADSORPTION   *See* ABSORPTION AND ADSORPTION.

AEROBE (er′ōb) An aerobe is an organism that uses the oxygen in the air in order to live and reproduce. In the process of respiration, an aerobe uses the oxygen mostly in order to break down food to obtain energy. (*See* RESPIRATION.) Many forms of life, including human beings, are aerobes. The major exceptions are certain microorganisms, such as some types of bacteria, fungi, and protozoans. Aerobic respiration converts food into energy more efficiently than the anaerobic process, called fermentation. *See also* ANAEROBE; FERMENTATION; MICROORGANISM.

A.J.C./E.R.L.

AERODYNAMICS (ar′ō dī nam′iks) is the study of gases in motion, including how air flows around objects. Aerodynamics is closely related to aeronautics because it studies the flight of airplanes and other machines that are heavier than air. The principles of aerodynamics also apply to the flow of air past buildings and bridges. (*See* AERONAUTICS.)

Four main forces act on a powered airplane in flight: lift, drag, gravity, and thrust. Lift and drag are results of airflow over the plane's surfaces.

Lift   The wings help lift the airplane. The wings' shape, angle of attachment, and area are what cause this lift. Seen in cross section, the wing has a rounded nose, a sharply curved upper surface, and a flatter bottom surface. Both surfaces taper to a sharp trailing edge. A body, such as the wing, designed to produce a desired effect in relation to the air surrounding it is called an airfoil. As the airplane flies, the air passing over the top of the wing has a greater distance to travel. Therefore, the air passing over the top of the wing must flow faster than the air flowing along the bottom of the wing. The pressure of the faster-moving air on top decreases. This creates a suction effect. At the same time, the pressure of the slower-moving air across the underside of the wing increases. These two forces—suction from above and pressure from below—lift the airplane as it moves through the air. (*See* AIRFOIL; BERNOULLI'S EFFECT.)

The angle at which the wing is attached to the body of the airplane is called the angle of incidence. The angle of incidence also has a part in lift. The front edge of the wing is tilted upward to increase the air pressure on the underside of the wing. The angle at which the air flow hits the wing is called the angle of attack. If the angle is increased, it increases lift. If the wing is tilted upward too much for a given speed, the airflow across the top of the wing breaks off. The lifting force of the wing stops. This is called a stall. If a stall occurs during flight, the airplane must be put into an immediate dive. Then it can pick up enough speed so that air can begin flowing across the top of the wing again. If the stall happens near the ground, the airplane may crash.

The shape of the airfoil, the total area of the wings, the angle of attack, the speed of airflow, and the density of the air all contribute to lift. Larger wings provide more lift. Increased speed also provides lift. Lift decreases at very high altitudes where the air is not dense enough to support an airfoil.

To climb, the pilot deflects the tail control surfaces, or elevators. When the rear edges of the elevators point up, the airflow on top pushes the tail down. This points the plane up.

To turn, the pilot moves the plane's rudder to one side. The air pressure pushes the whole tail in the opposite direction. This movement causes the plane's nose to move to the same side as the rudder. The pilot tips the wings of the airplane by raising the inside aileron, or spoiler, and lowering the outside aileron.

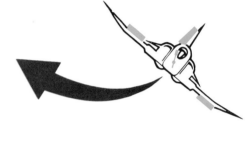

To dive, the pilot pushes the control column forward to deflect the elevators' rear edges downward. Air pressure then pushes the tail up.

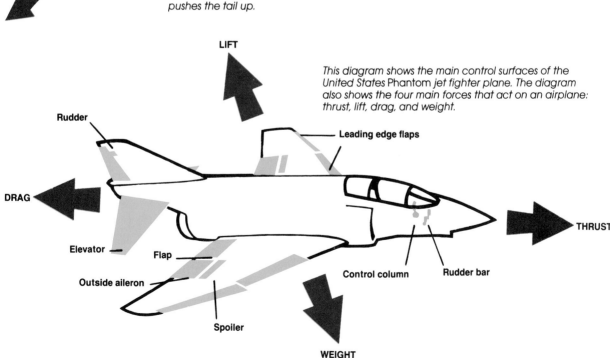

This diagram shows the main control surfaces of the United States Phantom *jet fighter plane. The diagram also shows the four main forces that act on an airplane: thrust, lift, drag, and weight.*

LIFT

Rudder

Leading edge flaps

DRAG

THRUST

Elevator

Flap

Control column

Rudder bar

Outside aileron

Spoiler

WEIGHT

Drag The force that fights against the forward progress of an airplane is called drag. If the shape of the body of the airplane is properly streamlined, the air will flow around it smoothly and cause little drag. A badly shaped body results in poor air flow and more drag. As a result, more energy is needed to push the airplane forward.

Skin friction, caused by roughness on the surface of the plane's body, also slows the forward progress of an airplane. Even the smallest bumps on the plane disturb the air. Disturbed air absorbs energy by friction. Skin friction can be reduced by making the surface of the plane's body very smooth. This is why airplanes are constantly cleaned and polished. Another kind of drag is called induced drag. Induced drag is caused by disturbed air at the

Civil engineers must take aerodynamic principles into account whenever they design a large bridge (above). Otherwise, wind damage could result. Airplane engineers test scale models of their designs in wind tunnels (below). Wind tunnels are large chambers with powerful fans that blow air through. The information gained from wind-tunnel tests is used to design better-performing and more efficient aircraft.

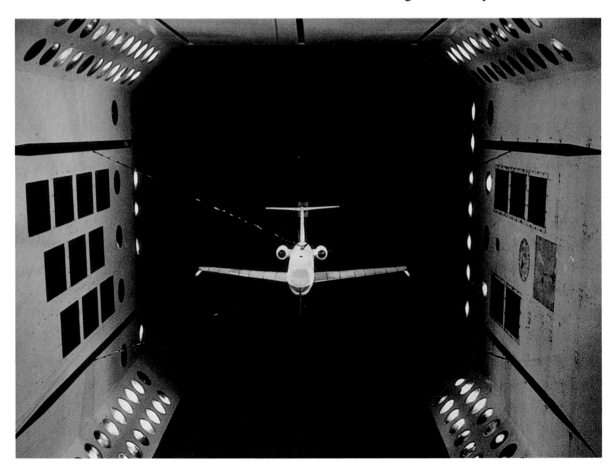

tips of the wings. At speeds faster than sound, shock waves develop over the surfaces of the wings. These reduce lift by disturbing the smooth flow of air over the wings and other surfaces. (*See* SUPERSONIC FLIGHT.)

Gravity Gravity is the force that pulls an airplane downward. The greater the mass, or weight, of the airplane, the more gravity will pull it down. Weight, as a force, is the opposite of lift.

Thrust Thrust is the force that propels an airplane forward. It is created by the engine, or engines, of the plane. Thrust is the opposite of drag.

Wind tunnels Airplane engineers test scale models of their designs in wind tunnels. These are large chambers with powerful fans blowing air through the tunnels in one direction. A model plane is suspended by wires or mounted on a string in the airflow. The designers watch the model through observation windows to see how it reacts to airflow. Measurements of all forces on the model are taken with sensitive instruments.

Wind tunnels are also used by automobile engineers and civil engineers to study the effects of airflow. Automobile shapes are designed to reduce drag. Some race cars even have airfoils that keep the car's front wheels on the track at high speeds. Designers of tall buildings and bridges also test models in wind tunnels to be sure the structures will be strong enough to resist high winds.

The theories of aerodynamics date back to Leonardo da Vinci, in the sixteenth century. He studied birds in flight. He even designed a flying machine that had birdlike wings. Otto Lilienthal provided further research with his study of unpowered flight in the 1880s. Samuel Langley published the first papers on aerodynamics in 1891. The Wright brothers flew the first powered airplane in 1903.

W.R.P./J.VP.

AERONAUTICS (ar'ə nŏt'iks) Aeronautics is the science of flight through the air. Aeronautical engineering is a general name for the study, design, building, and operating principles of aircraft.

Aviation is part of aeronautics. It refers most of the time to flight by heavier-than-air machines, such as the airplane and helicopter. Aerostatics is the part of aeronautics concerned with lighter-than-air machines, such as balloons and airships. Missiles that fly in the earth's atmosphere are also included in the field of aeronautics. However, long voyages outside the earth's atmosphere by crafts such as satellites belong to the field of astronautics. *See also* AERODYNAMICS; AIRPLANE; ASTRONAUTICS; DIRIGIBLE; MISSILE.

J.J.A./J.VP.

AEROSOL (ar'ə säl') An aerosol is a mist of tiny particles of liquid or solid suspended in air. Clouds and fog are examples of natural aerosols. Aerosols can also be human-made. Human-made aerosols include some forms of paints, perfumes, deodorants, and insecticides. Aerosols can be stored in spray cans that contain an active ingredient, such as paint or perfume, and a propellant. The active ingredient is a liquid, and the propellant is a liquefied gas. The propellant and the active ingredient mix in the can. The can is sealed under pressure. When the button on the top of the can is pressed, the propellant forces the mixture out. The propellant evaporates, leaving a fine spray of the active ingredient.

Until the late 1970s, the most common propellant used in aerosol products was a chlorofluorocarbon called Freon. Aerosol products are popular, and huge amounts of Freon were released into the atmosphere. Many scientists believe that Freon is dangerous because when it combines with the ozone in the atmosphere, the ozone layer is destroyed. For that reason, the use of Freon in aerosols was banned in 1978. Other propellants are now used. *See also* CHLOROFLUOROCARBON; OZONE.

M.E.; P.W./J.T.; L.W.

AEROSPACE (ar'ō spās') *Aerospace* refers to the region that includes everything from the surface of the earth outward. Scientists believe that the earth's atmosphere and outer space are one vast region. *Aerospace* is a term taken from the words *aeronautics* and *space*.

Aerospace also refers to the science of all flight within this region, which includes aeronautics and astronautics. One goal of aerospace science is to study the planets at close range. The science of astronomy is also part of aerospace.

The desire to develop air transportation and to explore space led to the aerospace industry. Some discoveries in this field are already part of everyday life. More than 200 million passengers use air transportation each year. Such transportation has proven to be safe, fast, and economical. Television programs and telephone calls from other continents are sent by satellites that orbit the earth. Other satellites provide accurate maps and weather forecasts. *See also* AERONAUTICS; ASTRONAUTICS; ASTRONOMY; SATELLITE; SPACE TRAVEL.

J.J.A./A.D.

AFRICAN VIOLET *See* VIOLETS AND PANSIES.

AGAR (äg'ər) Agar is a substance found in the cell walls of certain red algae. (*See* ALGAE.) When separated from the algae, agar is useful as a thickener. Agar absorbs up to twenty times its weight in water. Agar is used in cosmetic products, such as lipsticks and soaps, and in foods, such as ice cream and jelly. Since the late 1800s, scientists have used agar to study microorganisms, such as bacteria. Most microorganisms grow easily on agar when it is mixed with nutrients, such as sugar or starch. *See also* MICROORGANISM.

C.C./J.E.P.

AGASSIZ, LOUIS (1807-1873) Louis Agassiz was a Swiss-American naturalist responsible for many important scientific discoveries. He was born in Motiers, Switzerland, and studied medicine in various European schools. He never practiced medicine because he was more interested in nature. He became a professor of natural history at the University of Neuchatel in Switzerland. Agassiz traveled a great deal and studied fish fossils and the movement of glaciers. He was the first person

Louis Agassiz

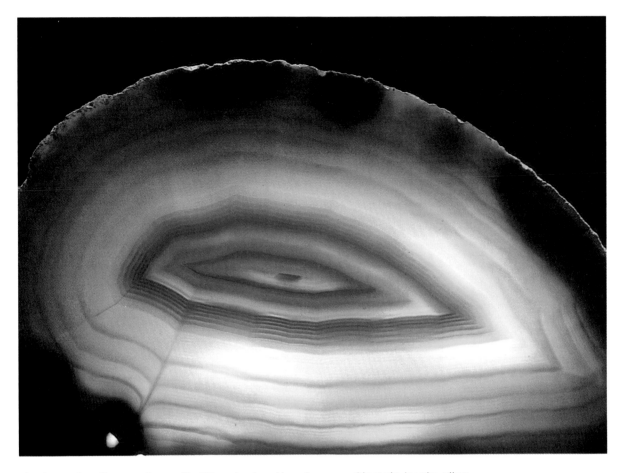

Agates, such as the one above with different-colored bands, are used to make jewelry, other ornaments, and marbles.

to propose the idea of continental glaciation. His idea described how, thousands of years ago, much of Europe, Asia, and North America was covered by huge sheets of ice. This ice cover was responsible for creating many of the valleys, lakes, and mountains that exist today. (*See* GLACIATION.)

In 1846, Professor Agassiz came to the United States. He was a very popular public figure and traveled around the country lecturing on natural history. He also taught at Harvard University. Agassiz continued to study glaciers and discovered evidence of a large prehistoric lake that covered parts of North Dakota, Minnesota, and Canada. This lake is now called Lake Agassiz.   S.R.G./D.G.F.

AGATE (ag′ət) Agate is a semiprecious mineral from the quartz family. An agate is a microcrystalline form of quartz, meaning the individual grains of quartz can only be seen with a microscope. Agates usually occur in bright solid colors. Sometimes an agate has bands or other patterns of colors running through it. (*See* QUARTZ.)

Agate probably gets its name from the Achates River in Sicily, where it was first found. Today, it can be found in many places in the world, including the western part of the United States. Agate is very hard. It is used to make decorative items, small implements, and marbles. Some cameos are cut from the onyx variety of agate. A cameo is an ornament showing a raised design in solid color against a lighter background. *See also* ONYX.

W.R.P./R.H.; E.W.L.

AGAVE (a gäv'ē) Agaves are a group of plants belonging to the agave family, Agavaceae. Agaves are found in Mexico and the southwestern United States. A waxy coating on their thick, leathery leaves prevents loss of water. This allows the plants to live in hot, dry areas.

The rosette of the Agave parviflora *is pictured.*

Agaves grow bunches of pointed, toothed leaves called rosettes. A flowing stem grows up from the middle of the rosette. Because agaves were once believed to take one hundred years to produce their first flowers, they have been called century plants. We now know that the plant's first flowers may appear between eight and forty years.

Agaves have many uses. For example, the leaves of one species are used in making sisal, a strong fiber used in rope. The roots of others have been used to make soap. S.R.G./M.H.S.

AGGLOMERATE (ə gläm'ə rət) Agglomerate is a dark, rough volcanic rock made up of hardened lava mixed with dust and ash, all of which are the products of a volcanic eruption. The volcano is also the source of the heat that serves to bind these materials together to form a rock. *See also* IGNEOUS ROCK. G.M.B./R.H.

AGRICULTURE (ag'ri kəl'chər) Agriculture, or farming, is the scientific practice of raising plants and animals as crops. (*See* CROP.) Farming includes some or all of the following four main activities: cultivating (preparing) the soil and planting, harvesting, and marketing the crop. Examples of crops raised for food include cattle, hogs, fruits, grains, and vegetables. The raising of fish, shellfish, or seaweed for food is called aquaculture. Other kinds of crops include trees raised for lumber or landscaping and cotton and silk raised for cloth. People who raise animals are often called ranchers or herders, rather than farmers.

Earliest agriculture Early humans were hunters and gatherers who moved from place to place in search of food. When people learned to plant and harvest food, they were able to stay in one place. This allowed the development of villages and the start of civilization. It is believed that farming began about 6000 B.C. in the area known today as Turkey and Israel. Knowledge of farming spread from that area to northern Africa. Wheat became the major food crop in northern Africa and throughout the Mediterranean region. Rice became the major food crop in the Far East. Corn became the major food crop in North and South America. These early farmers used simple tools to help them produce larger and healthier crops. Also about 6000 B.C., people in Europe and the Middle East learned to

Vegetable and fruit markets (top) make it possible for people who live in towns and cities to buy fresh produce directly from the farmers who raised it. Turkeys are a popular kind of poultry raised by farmers (bottom left). The ones shown here were bred to resemble those raised in colonial Virginia. Advancements in plant genetics have had an impact on the modern farm (bottom right) by producing breeds of corn and other grains that give high yields and are disease resistant.

capture, tame, and raise animals for food. This knowledge later spread to the Americas. Aquaculture is another early example of farming. Aquaculture was practiced in China as early as 4,000 years ago.

Modern agriculture In the 1800s, Gregor Mendel discovered how characteristics of plants and animals are inherited from their parents' genes. (*See* MENDEL, GREGOR.) This discovery opened new possibilities in the

Progress in science and technology has left its mark on the modern dairy farm. Today's dairy farmer milks cows and does many other chores by machine.

study of genetics. (*See* GENETICS.) By controlling which animals are bred or which seeds are planted, a farmer can achieve desired characteristics. (*See* BREEDING.) These characteristics include sweeter apples and leaner hogs. As another example, an ear of modern corn may have twice the number of kernels on it as an ear of wild corn.

Since the early 1900s, the use of the gasoline engine and special machines has greatly helped farmers. In developed countries, such as the United States, farmers no longer have to rely on hand tools or horses for planting, plowing, and harvesting. Farmers can grow and harvest large amounts of food quickly using tractors and combines. A tractor is a large machine used to pull other equipment. A combine is a machine that harvests grain. The combine largely replaced two machines called the reaper and the thresher in the early 1900s. The reaper cut the stalks, and the thresher separated the kernels of grain from the stalks. Advances in technology have helped agriculture in many other ways as well. Special buildings have been designed to house animals or store grain. Some large dairy farms have conveyors, or moving belts, that deliver food to each animal, mechanical milking machines, and mechanical floor scrapers for removing manure (animal waste). Electricity lights and heats barns. Electricity also keeps chicken eggs warm to help them hatch. Refrigeration keeps food from spoiling while it is being stored or delivered.

Modern agriculture involves branches of bacteriology, chemistry, climatology, engineering, and meteorology. (*See* BACTERIA; CHEMISTRY; CLIMATE; ENGINEERING; METEOROLOGY.) For example, chemists have developed products that control weeds, insect pests, and diseases. (*See* HERBICIDE; INSECTICIDE; PESTICIDE.) Agricultural engineers have designed tractors that use laser beams to guide the plowing of sloped land. Plowing with the help of laser beams helps control soil erosion. Weather information conveyed by satellites, photographs taken from airplanes, and computers help farmers decide when to plant crops and help them monitor the crops' progress. Farmers also use computers to receive information about crop prices.

Modern agriculture often involves diversified farming. A diversified farm raises different kinds of plants and/or animals. A diversified farmer may raise some crops that are not usually produced in his or her area, such as ginseng. (*See* GINSENG FAMILY.) Ginseng is added to such products as shampoos and soft drinks. Many people believe the root of the ginseng plant can cure illnesses. A farmer in the United States or the Soviet Union might also try practicing aquaculture. Aquaculture is mainly practiced today in China. A farmer can raise aquacultural products, such as fish, in an enclosure built on land or in natural bodies of water. Lobsters and oysters are examples of crops grown in salt water. Catfish and sturgeons are examples of crops grown in fresh water.

Thousands of fish are raised each year in these indoor pools. The water is continually filtered and recirculated.

Environmental concerns Modern agricultural practices have caused a rising number of environmental concerns. One of these practices is that of planting the same crop on the same piece of land every year. This practice is encouraged by U.S. government policies that award larger subsidies for certain crops, such as corn, cotton, soybeans, and wheat. A subsidy is a gift of money to a person or group whose efforts are helping the public. Planting the same crop year after year removes certain nutrients, such as nitrogen, from the soil. (*See* NITROGEN; NITROGEN CYCLE.) The practice of replacing nutrients with synthetic, or human-made, fertilizers has led to another concern. (*See* FERTILIZER.) Residues, or traces, of these fertilizers may remain on fruits, grains, and vegetables or run off into drinking water supplies. These residues may be poisonous to humans and other animals. Another environmental concern is the use of chemicals to kill insect pests. Over the years, certain pests may develop in such a way so that they are no longer harmed by the chemical. The chemical then has to be made stronger. If these chemicals are improperly used, they may pollute drinking water.

Soil erosion, or the loss of the top layer of soil due to wind or water, is another concern. (*See* EROSION.) Plowing has contributed to soil erosion. If the soil continues to be eroded, fertile farmland may become desertlike. However, techniques used today, such as strip cropping and contour plowing, help reduce erosion from rainwater on sloping land. In strip cropping, grass is planted between strips of crops to slow the flow of rainwater. In contour plowing, the farmer plows along the curve of the slope, rather than up and down. This slows the flow of rainwater.

The raising of animals, such as cattle, also affects the environment. For example, cattle farming requires large amounts of water. It takes 2,500 gal. [9,460 liters] of water to produce 1 lb. [0.4536 kg] of beef. However, it takes only 60 gal. [227 liters] of water to produce 1 lb. [0.4536 kg] of wheat. Also, many forests in the United States and tropical rain forests around the world have been chopped down and burned to clear land for crops and livestock. Some scientists believe the chopping down of forests will affect the worldwide environment.

Alternative agriculture Some farmers have started using alternative methods of farming along with conventional methods. The goal of alternative agriculture (often called sustainable agriculture) is to produce high-quality crops at a profit while protecting the environment. A farmer practicing alternative agriculture also tries to use the resources he or she has on the farm, such as manure, instead of relying on purchased resources, such as synthetic fertilizers. One method of alternative agriculture is planting different crops in the same field each year to preserve and even add nutrients to the soil. This practice is called crop rotation. Crop rotation helps preserve nutrients because every crop takes different amounts of different nutrients out of the soil. Another method of alternative agriculture is called integrated pest management. This method limits the amount of synthetic insecticides and pesticides applied to a field. Instead, natural enemies are also used to fight off pests. (*See* BIOLOGICAL CONTROL.) Farmers are also leaving harvest debris, such as stalks, in the fields. This debris fertilizes the soil, helps control erosion, and provides shelter for wildlife.

One way to achieve some of the goals of alternative agriculture is through organic farming. In organic farming, chemicals are not used. Biodynamic farming is a branch of organic farming. Biodynamic farming attempts to restore the nutrients in soil by adding compost, manure, and mulch. (*See* COMPOST; MULCH.) The practice of permaculture is another approach to alternative agriculture. This practice tries to create an efficient ecological system on the farm. It involves managing crops, land, water, and animals so that both the products and waste from each part of the system are used. For example, hogs not only produce meat, but also manure for fertilizer. A pond may provide water to raise fish, irrigate land, water livestock, and act as a fire barrier.

Agriculture and society The world's population is growing rapidly. There are more people to feed today, but less land for farming. Factories, office buildings, and homes are

Increasing amounts of land are being used to raise livestock, such as these beef cattle.

often constructed on what could be good cropland. Land used to graze livestock is also increasing. This is in spite of the fact that studies show that peas or beans yield ten times as much protein per acre as livestock. In addition, fewer people are farming now. Many farmers' children move away to get other jobs. Other people no longer farm because they cannot make enough money. There is a trend for large corporations to own farms. However, the majority of American farms are still family owned. Producing enough food and providing farmers with a profit while staying in harmony with the environment is a constant challenge.   C.C./T.L.G.; J.E.P.

This agronomist is artificially pollinating corn plants in an effort to develop improved breeds. Agronomists work with crops to do such things as improve their yield, make them disease resistant, and make them able to withstand unfavorable growing conditions.

AGRONOMY (ə grän′ə mē) Agronomy is the branch of agriculture that deals with the study of field crops. Most agronomy is concerned with aiding production of the world's ten major food crops—barley, corn, millet, potatoes, rice, sorghum, soybeans, sweet potatoes, wheat, and cassava. Cassava is a small shrub grown in Africa, India, Indonesia, and South America. The roots and leaves of the cassava plant are eaten.

Agronomists design new plant breeds that have higher yields or better nutritional quality. (*See* BREEDING.) Agronomists also advise farmers on ways to control weeds and insect pests without harming the environment. *See also* AGRICULTURE.   C.C./J.E.P.

AIDS Acquired Immune Deficiency Syndrome, or AIDS, is a disease that affects the body's immune system by destroying its ability to fight many other diseases. There is no known cure for AIDS. It always results in

death. AIDS victims do not die of AIDS itself. Rather, they die of some other disease, such as pneumonia or cancer, that their bodies cannot resist.

Acquired means that AIDS is not an inherited disease. Instead, it is caused by a virus called HIV (human immuno-deficiency virus). The virus is often called the AIDS virus as well. Viruses are microscopic organisms, some of which cause disease. The AIDS virus lives in certain body fluids such as blood, blood plasma, and semen. *Immune Deficiency* means that those systems that normally protect the body from disease do not work properly. *Syndrome* means that AIDS patients usually show physical symptoms resulting from the disease. AIDS is suspected when certain serious infections occur that usually only develop when the HIV virus is present. Tests are then performed to see if the person actually has the HIV virus. Sometimes, an individual can be infected with the AIDS virus but will not actually develop

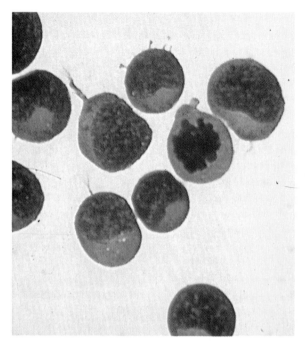 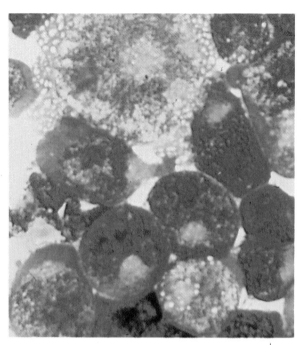

Normal, healthy T-cells are shown above left. The T-cells pictured above right have been infected by the Acquired Immune Deficiency Syndrome (AIDS) virus.

AIDS. This is known as ARC (AIDS-related complex). People with ARC may have fever, fatigue, diarrhea, and weight loss.

Most AIDS and ARC victims catch the disease through sexual contact with someone infected with the AIDS virus. Others are infected by using hypodermic needles or syringes contaminated with the AIDS virus to inject themselves with drugs. In the past, small numbers of people have gotten the disease from AIDS-contaminated blood transfusions. Also, each year, a growing number of children are born with AIDS that they catch from their mothers' infected blood.

Once in the body, the AIDS virus enters the bloodstream. There, it kills many of a special kind of white blood cell—called the helper T-cell—that helps the body protect itself against infection.

Nonsexual contact between people does not spread the AIDS virus. There are no known cases in which AIDS has been spread because of eating, kissing, coughing, sneezing, playing, shaking hands, or working with someone who has AIDS.

Drugs have been developed that may help people with AIDS live longer. These drugs help fight off the infections that the body cannot. Scientists hope to develop drugs that prevent AIDS. At this time, the only way to prevent AIDS is to avoid the kind of behavior that spreads the disease. One such behavior is using infected needles or syringes. Another risky behavior is having sexual contact with an infected person, or a person who thinks he or she might be infected, without using a condom.

The number of AIDS cases is rising rapidly and has become a major health crisis in many parts of the United States and the rest of the world. There is little evidence that the worldwide AIDS epidemic is being controlled. Many experts fear that AIDS will remain a major health problem for many years. *See also*

BLOOD; BLOOD TRANSFUSION; COCAINE; DISEASE; IMMUNITY; VIRUS.   P.Q.F./L.V.C.

AIR is the mixture of gases that surrounds the earth. It is invisible and tasteless and has no smell. Air extends great distances above the earth. One half of the air, by weight, is within 3.5 mi. [5.63 km] of the earth's surface. The other half is spread over hundreds of miles beyond that. The layer of air surrounding the earth makes life possible. It is prevented from escaping into space by gravity. (*See* GAS; GRAVITY .)

Composition of air Nitrogen makes up about 78 percent of the air, oxygen 21 percent, and argon almost 1 percent. More accurately, these gases make up 99.77 percent of the air. The remaining gases include tiny percentages of carbon dioxide, helium, krypton, neon, ozone, and xenon.

The amount of carbon dioxide in the air varies from place to place. The highest amounts of carbon dioxide are found in cities and in places such as closed rooms. Carbon dioxide is a very important gas. It is used by green plants in photosynthesis. (*See* PHOTOSYN-THESIS.) Air also contains moisture in the form of water vapor, which is a gas. The amount of water vapor in the air depends upon the temperature. Warm air can hold much more water vapor than cold air. Dust in the air serves as a center around which water vapor collects. This dust may come from dust storms, automobile exhaust, or smoke from factories. Dust also includes plant pollen, bacteria, and tiny salt particles. When warm air cools, it may reach the dew point. The dew point is the temperature at which the air is holding all the water it possibly can. The term *relative humidity* is used to describe the amount of water vapor in the air compared with the amount of water vapor the air can hold at a given temperature. When air reaches the dew point, the relative humidity is 100 percent. (*See* DEW POINT; HUMIDITY.)

Cooling may also cause water vapor to surround specks of dust to form tiny water droplets. A mass of these droplets forms a cloud. If the conditions are right, clouds may produce rain or snow. High up in the atmosphere, where it is very cold, water vapor may become ice crystals by a process called subli-mination. A mass of ice crystals forms cirrus clouds high in the atmosphere. (*See* ATMO-SPHERE; CLOUD.)

The air surrounding the earth is divided into layers. From the earth's surface to about 7 mi. [11.3 km] up is the troposphere. This is where almost all of the earth's weather occurs. Above this layer are the stratosphere and the ionosphere. The exosphere is where the air thins out into space.

Air weight and pressure The force of gravity holds the air and gives it weight. At sea level, 1 cu. ft. [0.03 cu. m] of air weighs 0.081 lb. [0.037 kg]. However, the hundreds of miles of air above the earth weigh so much that the total force on 10.7 sq. ft. [1 sq. m] of surface is about 22,604 lb. [10,253 kg]. Air pressure is the measure of the force of air on a given area. Air pressure at the earth's surface is equal in all directions. People do not feel this pressure because their bodies are supported by equal pressure on the inside. In the atmosphere, air pressure varies and is measured by instruments called barometers. Weather forecasts are based partly on changes in barometric pressure. (*See* BAROMETER; WEATHER.)

Air pressure decreases above sea level. At 18,000 ft. [5,486 m] high, the pressure is half as great as it is at the earth's surface. For this reason, airplanes have pressurized cabins to make flying more comfortable. Air pressure is used as a force in pumps. Air pressure is what keeps automobile tires from going flat.

Air resistance People move through air easily, as they do in walking. However, a piece of paper dropped in the air floats slowly to the ground. The falling of the paper is slowed down because of the air resistance acting on the large surface area of the paper. A bullet moves quickly through the air. Its smooth surface and pointed end reduce air resistance.

The wind that is moving these sailboats along is an indication that the air is in constant motion.

Air motion Although it may seem to be motionless on a hot summer's day, air is never still. Molecules of air are in constant motion. Large masses of air also move. This motion is measured as wind. The sun provides the energy that causes the air to move. Because air is always moving, the weather is always changing. (*See* AIR MASS; WIND.)

Air pollution Air pollution is a serious problem in the United States and other countries.

Coal-powered electric power plants such as this one are one of the major sources of air pollution. The sulfur and nitrogen they release into the atmosphere are one of the most important causes of acid rain.

Pollutants enter the air from many sources. Automobiles, electric-power plants, factories, and other sources release chemicals into the atmosphere. Many of these chemicals are harmful to the environment.

For example, the sulfur and nitrogen released in the smoke of many coal-burning electric-power plants combine with the water in the atmosphere to produce acid rain. Acid rain is harmful to plants and animals. (*See* ACID RAIN.) Industrial processes that involve the production of coke (coal that has been heated to a high temperature without air) release a chemical called benzene into the atmosphere. Benzene is known to affect the blood and can cause severe leukemia (a form of cancer) and anemia (a condition in which the number of healthy red blood cells in the human body falls below normal). (*See* BENZENE.) Other chemicals, called chlorofluorocarbons, are used as refrigerants in air conditioners and refrigerators and to make plastic foams. When released into the atmosphere, they destroy the ozone layer in the upper stratosphere. (*See* ATMOSPHERE; CHLOROFLUOROCARBON; OZONE.) The exhaust from automobiles combines with oxygen in the atmosphere to form smog. (*See* SMOG.) Exhaust also contains carbon dioxide, which is the main gas responsible for the greenhouse effect. In the greenhouse effect, pollution in the atmosphere helps trap the sun's heat above the earth. This may cause the earth's temperature to rise. (*See* GREENHOUSE EFFECT.)

In recent years, the federal, state, and local governments have worked together to try to control air pollution. The federal government issues air-quality standards. The state and local governments must then enforce measures so these standards are met. One major step by the federal government to control pollution was the 1970 Clean Air Act. This act set limits on the amount of pollution that could be released in automobile exhaust, factories, and electric-power plants. A new Clean Air Act became law in 1990. It requires greatly lowered levels of pollution from automobiles, factories, and power plants. It also requires the use of reformulated fuels and gasohol (containing methanol) and requires the sale of cars that use the new fuels. *See also* GASOLINE; POLLUTION.

J.J.A.; P.Q.F./E.W.L.; C.R.; L.W.

AIR-CUSHION VEHICLE An air-cushion vehicle, also called a Hovercraft or surface-effect ship, hovers over the earth on a cushion of air. It can travel over any fairly flat surface, either ground or water.

Most air-cushion vehicles are used for traveling over water. They can move very fast, and some have a top speed of 90 mi. per hour [150 km per hour]. Air-cushion vehicles can travel at these high speeds because they do not move through the water. An ordinary ship travels more slowly. It is slowed down by friction between the hull and the water. (*See*

FRICTION.) In an air-cushion vehicle, air is sucked in through the top of the vehicle by a large fan. The air is then blown through nozzles to the bottom of the craft. Here it forms a cushion of air.

Many air-cushion vehicles are surrounded by a "skirt" that reaches down to the water. The "skirt" is called a plenum. It helps keep the air inside the cushion. This allows the vehicle to ride higher out of the water, above waves that are fairly high.

The diagram below shows the fan of a Hovercraft bringing in air, which is then directed to the bottom of the craft. The diagram at right shows the underside of the craft, with its air openings. Notice the tail fins.

Air-cushion vehicles travel by means of propellers driven by engines. The propellers on the vehicles face backwards. By swiveling the propellers, an operator can steer the vehicle. Some air-cushion vehicles have large vertical tail fins and are steered by turning the fins to either side. Because of the high speed at which they can travel, air-cushion vehicles are very useful for carrying passengers and freight between ports. They are only used for fairly short distances, since they cannot, as yet, travel in rough seas. Air-cushion vehicles are also very useful for traveling over swamps.

M.E./R.W.L.

AIRFOIL (er′fôil′) An airfoil is a body, such as an airplane wing, that interacts with airflow to produce a desired effect. For example, as an airplane moves through the air, the air divides to pass above and below its wings.

Each wing has a curved upper surface and a flatter bottom surface. This design causes the air moving above the wing to move faster than air moving below. Fast-moving air has less pressure than slow-moving air, creating a suction effect. (*See* BERNOULLI'S EFFECT.) The combination of suction from above and pressure from below lifts the airplane. *See also* AERODYNAMICS.

P.W./L.W.

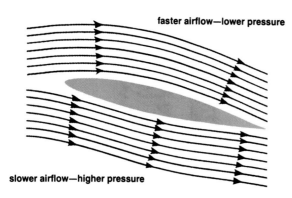

The diagram shows a cross section of an airplane wing and how it serves as an airfoil. Suction from above the wing and pressure from below the wing combine to lift the airplane.

AIR MASS An air mass is a huge body of air. It often extends 1,000 mi. [1,600 km] or more across a given area. The higher parts of an air mass are colder than the lower parts. The temperature of air decreases with height. On the same level, the air in one part of the air mass is about the same temperature as the air in other parts of the same mass.

There are four main types of air masses: continental polar, continental tropical, maritime polar, and maritime tropical. Continental air masses form over land, while maritime air masses form over the sea. Continental polar air masses are cold and dry. Continental tropical air masses are warm and dry. Maritime polar air masses are cool and moist. Maritime tropical air masses are warm and moist.

A cold air mass is colder than the ground surface over which it moves, and a warm air mass is warmer than the ground surface. Cold air weighs more than warm air. Therefore, a cold air mass exerts greater pressure on the earth than a warm air mass does. Cooler air tends to move toward the warmer air because of the difference in pressure.

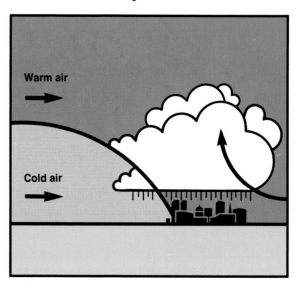

When a cold air mass meets a warm air mass, the cold air tends to push the warm air up. The warm air cools as it rises, causing clouds and precipitation.

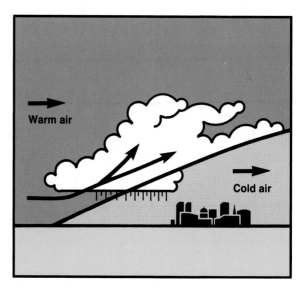

If wind causes a warm air mass to overtake a cold air mass, the lighter warm air slides up over the cold air. Clouds and precipitation form.

When a cold air mass meets a warm one, the cold air tends to run under the warm air instead of mixing with it. The line along which this occurs is called a cold front. (*See* COLD FRONT.) As the warm air is pushed up, it expands and cools. This causes cloud formations and precipitation, such as rain or snow. Precipitation occurs because warm air holds more water vapor than cool air does. As the warm air grows cooler, the water vapor leaves the air. (*See* CONDENSATION.) It falls to earth in the form of rain, sleet, snow, or a combination of the three. If wind movements cause a warm air mass to overtake a cold air mass, the warm air, weighing less, slides up over the cold. Clouds and precipitation are formed. This is called a warm front. (*See* WARM FRONT.)

When an air mass is moving very slowly, its moisture content and temperature are affected by the surface below it. For example, an air mass may take on the coldness of a polar region or the heat of the tropics. The region where an air mass takes on its temperature and moisture is called its source region. The depth to which an air mass is changed by its source region depends upon the length of time the air stays in the source region. It also depends upon the difference between the temperature of the air and that of the underlying surface.

Weather maps use symbols, such as *cP* for continental polar, *cT* for continental tropical, *mP* for maritime polar, and *mT* for maritime tropical, to identify air masses. Such symbols explain where the air mass began, the direction it is taking, and the type of surface over which it is moving. As an air mass moves from one surface to another, it can change from a warm air mass (*w*) to a cold air mass (*k*).

Across the United States, the general movement of air masses is from west to east. A cold air mass moves faster than a warm one. A cold air mass may average 500 to 700 mi. [800 to 1,120 km] in a day. The weather depends on the type of air mass and on the action between two or more air masses. With just one air mass, the weather is about the same throughout the area it covers. Differences are caused by changes in the surfaces below, such as lakes, mountains, and valleys. *See also* WEATHER.   J.J.A./D.W.K.; C.R.

AIRPLANE   An airplane is a heavier-than-air vehicle with fixed wings that flies. Before an airplane can fly, a force greater than its own weight must be created. This force is called lift. An airplane obtains lift from the design of its wings. (*See* AIRFOIL.) There are airplanes with and without engines. The engines provide forward motion by a force called thrust. (*See* AERODYNAMICS.) Unpowered airplanes have to be brought into the air by tow before they can glide to earth.

There are three main categories of airplanes: military, commercial, and private. Military planes include fighters, bombers,

The United States Navy's Blue Angels, one of the world's finest precision-flying groups, uses military fighter planes.

transports, and trainers. Most are powered by gas turbine jet engines. (*See* ENGINE; JET PROPULSION; TURBINE.) Commercial planes include passenger and cargo planes used by airlines, as well as planes developed for special uses. Most large commercial planes are powered by jet engines. Some still have piston engines with propellers. Between these two types are turboprop airplanes, which use jet engines and propellers. Private planes are those owned by individuals and companies. They are usually small, carrying from one to six people. Most are powered by one or two piston engines or jet engines.

History The first attempts to fly were made with balloons. (*See* BALLOON.) The Montgolfier brothers succeeded in making the first balloon flight in 1783, in France, using heated air. Starting one hundred years later, Otto Lilienthal of Germany made two thousand flights in gliders over a twenty-year period. A glider is an airplane without an engine. Gliders are towed aloft by a winch and cable, or by a powered airplane. Then they are released. They depend upon rising and shifting air currents for lift. In 1903, Orville Wright of the United States made the world's first powered flight at Kitty Hawk, North Carolina. (*See* WRIGHT BROTHERS.)

The need for military planes in World War I (1914-1918) speeded up airplane development. Progress was rapid. By World War II (1939-1945), the airplane had become a major weapon. Air speeds in the 300 to 400 m.p.h. [480 to 640 kph] range were common. Jet-powered planes were introduced in the late 1940s. They have since come into wide use. Some military and commercial jet planes now fly at supersonic speeds (faster than the speed of sound, which is 760 m.p.h. or 1,220

kph, and is called Mach 1). The French *Concorde* passenger plane flies at Mach 2.2 (2.2 times the speed of sound, 1,672 m.p.h. or 2,684 kph). It is the fastest commercial plane in service. (*See* MACH; SUPERSONIC FLIGHT.)

Other recent developments in airplane design have been VTOL and STOL planes. VTOL (vertical takeoff and landing) planes lift straight up off the ground in a horizontal position, like helicopters, before flying forward. STOL (short takeoff and landing) planes have powerful engines and high-lift wings that enable them to take off and land on very short runways.

Airplane parts The body of an airplane, which contains the pilot cockpit and the passenger compartment, is called the fuselage. The wings and tail are attached to it. The engine, or engines, may be mounted in the fuselage or on the wings. Sometimes they are attached beneath the wings on finlike devices called pylons. The landing gear consists of heavy wheels with shock-absorbing supports. The landing gear is folded up into the plane during flight to reduce air resistance, which would slow the plane. Small private planes often have landing gears that cannot be moved.

The tail surfaces at the rear of the plane and the wings have movable parts that control the forces on the airplane and the direction of flight. The vertical part of the tail is called the rudder. The horizontal parts, which are like small wings, are called the elevators. Movable parts on the wings include the ailerons, which help control direction. Flaps can be lowered to reduce speed and to increase lift. Spoilers, on top of the wings, help reduce lift if required. All the movable parts are controlled by the pilot from the control center, or flight deck, of the plane.

Bi-wing aircraft are popular with stunt pilots, crop dusters, and aircraft hobbyists because such planes are easy to maneuver.

Wing design varies. Low-speed planes need large, thick wings to achieve sufficient lift. High-speed planes require only small, thin wings. Wings project out at right angles to the fuselage in low-speed planes. They are swept back in a V shape in high-speed planes to reduce drag.

Large passenger planes contain seats for the passengers, kitchens for serving food, and toilets. Baggage is usually stored in spaces below the passenger cabin. The cabin and flight deck areas are pressurized (that is, the air pressure is kept normal) to allow people to breathe at the altitudes where planes fly. (*See* AIR.)

Airplane engines Gas turbine jet engines and piston engines that turn propellers are the two main sources of power for airplanes. Some jet engines also turn propellers. These are called turboprops. The propeller spins at high speed and creates a lower pressure in front of itself. This sucks the airplane forward. The gas turbine jet engines take in air at the front end, mix it with fuel, and compress (squeeze) it. The mixture burns, and the hot, expanded gases drive the turbine for the compressor and come out the back end at high speed. This provides thrust, or a pushing effect. Turboprop engines combine both methods.

Jet engines create less vibration than piston engines. They are more efficient at high speeds and altitudes. They use kerosene, a fuel that is cheaper than gasoline.

Airplane instruments Modern airplanes are complicated machines. Pilots need many gauges and electronic aids to help fly them. The flight deck of a large passenger plane contains many indicator dials and warning lights. One of the most important instruments is the altimeter. (*See* ALTIMETER.) This tells the pilot how high the plane is off the ground. The air speed indicator measures the plane's speed. The artificial horizon shows the position of the plane relative to the horizon. The turn-and-bank indicator shows how much, if at all, the plane is turning and tilting. In dense clouds and fog, a pilot would not always know which way the plane is heading if it were not for this instrument. A gyrocompass and various radio devices are necessary for navigation. (*See* GYROSCOPE; NAVIGATION.)

Most large planes also have an automatic pilot. This is a device operated by a computer. It will fly the plane without the pilot's touching the controls. These autopilots can even control takeoffs and landings. The flight deck also contains many gauges and meters that tell the pilot whether the many pieces of equipment on the plane are operating properly. They measure fuel level, oil pressure, temperatures, thrust, cabin pressure, and electric current. Indicators show whether the landing gear is up or down. The radio equipment allows the pilot to talk to ground controllers and to receive navigation signals.

Airplane construction Early airplanes were made of wood frames covered by fabric and held in shape by wire. After World War I, airplane designers started to use lightweight metals such as aluminum, titanium, and magnesium alloys. A thin skin of metal was riveted into place over metal ribs. Strong epoxy glues are now used for some joints, instead of rivets. As planes grew in size, they became heavier. More powerful engines were developed in order to fly the heavier planes.

The use of metals brings with it a problem called metal fatigue. Stress and vibration in flight can cause metal parts eventually to

The manufacture of today's advanced, high-performance aircraft is complex and precise. Aircraft designs are tested thoroughly before the planes are manufactured. This is done to make sure that the finished product will be safe.

break up. Airplanes must be constantly checked for signs of this trouble. Defective parts must be renewed by aircraft maintenance people. Designers test scale models in wind tunnels, before the full-sized planes are built. Reactions of the models to high-speed air streams give good indications how full-sized planes will react in flight. This approach, which allows flaws to be corrected before manufacturing, helps save a great deal of money. It also helps make airplanes safer.

W.R.P./E.H.G.; F.J.M.; J.VP.

AIRPORT An airport is a place where airplanes arrive and depart. Passengers leave and arrive on the airplanes, and cargo is loaded and unloaded. Large, jet-powered airplanes require long runways for takeoffs and landings. Big terminal buildings are necessary to handle thousands of passengers and their baggage. The largest airports cover thousands of acres. Hundreds of planes arrive and depart daily. All this traffic must be carefully controlled to avoid delays and accidents. This is done from a control tower. The tower stands high above the ground. Air-traffic controllers, inside the tower, must be able to guide airplanes through their takeoffs and landings.

Large airports are often like small cities. Many have post offices, banks, hotels, restaurants, offices, and many kinds of shops. Airports also have their own fire and police departments, fuel storage tanks, repair workshops, and storage hangars. Some companies even have their shipping warehouses located at airports.

One of the largest airports in the world is in Grapevine, Texas, midway between the cities of Dallas and Fort Worth. This airport covers 18,000 acres [7,200 hectares]. Its five terminals can handle the arrivals and depar-

tures of ninety jumbo jets at the same time. O'Hare International Airport, in Chicago, is the busiest airport in the world. It handles about 56 million passengers a year.

Small airports that are used only by private airplanes usually cover 50 to 100 acres [20 to 40 hectares]. They do not need all the buildings and services of a large airport. The control tower may be just a small room in a building at ground level.

Loaded with passengers and their baggage, this airplane will soon move to a runway to take off.

Runways Today's big jet planes weigh hundreds of tons. They move along runways at speeds of over 100 m.p.h. [160 kph]. When they land, they hit the runways hard. The runways take a great deal of pounding and must be made of concrete or asphalt. They must have a solid foundation and a surface that prevents skidding.

Airplanes take off into the wind in order to get better lift. They also land into the wind in order to have better control as they slow down. (*See* AERODYNAMICS.) Most airports have runways pointing in different directions. This means that there are always runways on which airplanes can go into the wind as they take off and land.

Heavily loaded passenger jets need long runways to gather enough speed to leave the ground. Runways at some large airports are longer than 10,000 ft. [3,000 m].

At night, lights lining the runways shine brightly so that pilots can find them easily. A system of flashing guide lights is set up beyond the runway to help pilots land safely.

Air-traffic controllers, stationed in a tower at the airport, direct the movement of aircraft that are in the air as well as on the ground.

Control towers People who work in control towers are called air-traffic controllers. They direct the movements of all planes on the ground and in the air by keeping track of them on large radar screens. Air-traffic controllers tell a pilot, by radio, when and where to taxi or pilot the plane down the runway. At busy hours, when many planes have to take off, as many as fifteen jets may have to wait in line to take their turn.

Electronic equipment is used to guide airplanes. Long-range radar is used to keep track of planes far away from the airport. This radar is called Ground Control Approach (GCA). When the airplane gets within a few miles of the runway, the air-traffic controller begins to use Precision Approach Radar

(PAR). This allows the controller to guide the airplane to within 0.25 mi. [0.4 km] of the runway. At that point, the pilot completes the landing. Another electronic aid used in bad weather is the Instrument Landing System (ILS). In this system, radio transmitters located near the runway send guidance signals to the airplane. These signals tell the pilot how to steer the plane for the final approach to the runways. Today, there are also electronic microwave landing systems (MLS) that can land the plane fully automatically.

Terminal buildings Terminal buildings vary in size and shape. Most of them are quite large. More than 228 million people fly on airlines in America each year. Every passenger must pass through terminals. Long, covered walkways lead from the center of some terminals to the gates where airplanes are boarded. At some airports, buses are used to transport passengers to their airplanes. Passengers arriving from another country must pass through customs and passport control. Customs officials check the incoming baggage for taxable items. They also check to be sure no forbidden items are brought into the country. Passport officials check the passports of passengers for personal identification.

Passengers are not allowed to bring guns, knives, or other weapons onto a passenger airplane. Before boarding, they must walk through a detector that triggers a special signal if they are carrying anything made of metal. Luggage is also examined for weapons. This is done to ensure the safety of the passengers.   W.R.P./J.VP.

ALBATROSS (al′bə trós′) The albatross is a large seabird that belongs to the family Diomedeidae. It is found mainly south of the

ALB

equator. The albatross has a long, heavy beak and long, narrow wings that allow it to soar on the wind, seemingly without effort, for hours. The largest species is the wandering albatross, which has a wingspan of more than 11 ft. [3.4 m] and a body 4 ft. [1.2 m] long.

Albatrosses have difficulty beginning each flight. They need some wind and must run along the ground or paddle with their webbed feet across the water for a long time before being able to stay in the air.

S.R.G./L.S.

ALBINO (al bī′nō) An albino is an animal or plant that is unable to produce pigment (coloring matter) in its cells. Albinism is an inherited condition. (*See* GENE; HEREDITY.) Because many animals rely on pigment for protection from the sun and for protective coloration, albino animals are at a definite disadvantage in the wild. (*See* PROTECTIVE COLORATION.)

Albino animals rarely survive long enough to reproduce.

There are albinos in almost every race of human beings. Many albinos are complete (or true) albinos. They have pinkish white skin and white hair. Their eyes appear pink because of the color of the blood vessels. In a person with normal coloring, the pigment of the iris (usually brown or blue) blocks out the color of the blood vessels. (*See* EYE AND VISION.) Because other, light-absorbing pigments are also lacking, an albino is extremely sensitive to bright light such as sunlight.

Some people are partial albinos and lack pigment in some, but not all, tissues and organs. Some animals are also partial albinos. Some, though not all, plants with white flowers are partial albinos. A complete albino plant lacks even the green pigment chlorophyll. As a result, it is unable to photosynthesize, and dies shortly after food supplies in the

An albino animal cannot produce pigment in its cells. This albino rat is known as a complete albino. It has pinkish white skin, white hair, and pink eyes.

seed are used up. (*See also* CHLOROPHYLL; GENETICS; METABOLISM; PHOTOSYNTHESIS; PIGMENTATION.) A.J.C./E.R.L.

ALCHEMY (al′kə mē) Alchemy was an early form of chemistry. It was widely practiced during the Middle Ages. It developed from the ideas of ancient philosophers, such as Aristotle.

An alchemist used chemicals to try to change one thing into another. Alchemists thought that some metals were more "perfect" than others. They considered gold to be the most perfect metal of all. They tried to discover a substance that would make metals more and more perfect. They hoped that the metal would then turn into gold. They called the substance that would do this the philosopher's stone. They thought that if they took the philosopher's stone themselves, they would become better people. They also tried to discover the elixir of life. This was a medicine that was supposed to make people live forever.

Alchemy was related to religion, magic, and astrology. (*See* ASTROLOGY.) The sun, moon, and planets were linked with different metals. For example, alchemists linked gold with the sun and silver with the moon. People lost faith in alchemy in the 1600s. It is now thought to be unscientific. However, the alchemists' methods of heating and mixing substances led to modern chemistry. M.E./R.W.L.

ALCOHOL (al′kə hȯl′) Alcohol in its most common form is a clear, colorless liquid. It burns and evaporates easily. It has a burning taste. Alcohols are made from chemicals found in living things. They all have hydroxyl (OH) groups that are connected to carbon atoms.

The simplest alcohol is methanol, or methyl alcohol. This poisonous substance is commonly called wood alcohol. It once was produced from wood but now is produced mostly from methane. (*See* METHANE.) Its molecules consist of a methyl group (CH_3) connected to a hydroxyl group (OH). Its formula is CH_3OH. Ethanol, or ethyl alcohol, is commonly called grain alcohol. Its formula is C_2H_5OH.

Ethyl alcohol is used in alcoholic beverages, such as beer, wine, and liquor. The alcohol used in such beverages is produced by fermenting grains, such as barley, corn, and rye; fruits, such as grapes; or vegetables, such as potatoes. Ethyl alcohol is also used in stains, lacquers, and varnishes; as a solvent; and as a source of other chemicals. Sometimes, ethyl alcohol is combined with gasoline to make a fuel called gasohol. Methyl alcohol also may be used to make gasohol. (*See* GASOLINE.) Most methyl alcohol is converted to formaldehyde, a chemical used in making plastics. Methyl alcohol is also used as an antifreeze and in the making of paints and varnishes. It is used in combination with other chemicals as well. Other kinds of alcohols include isopropyl, glycol, and glycerol. Isopropyl alcohol is used in producing acetone (an industrial solvent), in the making of cosmetics, and as a rubbing alcohol. Glycol is used as antifreeze. Glycerol, or glycerin, is used as a softener in foods. It is also used in cosmetics, in medicines, and in nitroglycerin, an explosive used in making gunpowder and dynamite. J.J.A./T.L.G.; J.M.

ALCOHOLISM (al′kə hȯ′liz′əm) Alcoholism is a disease having to do with the overuse of alcoholic drinks. Such drinks include whiskey, gin, rum, vodka, bourbon, wine, and beer.

Some people can drink alcoholic beverages without serious harm. Other people become addicted to them. These people are called alcoholics. They depend on alcohol to help them ignore problems they cannot solve. They use alcohol in order to relax. If they do not have alcohol regularly, they may experience withdrawal symptoms. Withdrawal symptoms occur because, over time, the alcohol becomes necessary for the body's chemical processes to work. Withdrawal symptoms vary. Alcoholics may feel weak and tired. They may shake and perspire freely. Sometimes they vomit, run a fever, or hallucinate, seeing things that do not really exist. There are more than ten million alcoholics in the United States, making alcoholism one of the major diseases in the country. Alcoholism can help lead to diseases of the circulatory system, nervous system, liver, pancreas, stomach, and immune system. Many alcoholics are undernourished. Pregnant women who use too much alcohol may give birth to babies who have birth defects.

Alcohol acts as a depressant. A depressant dulls the parts of the brain that control speech, the emotions, judgment, and bodily movement. Because alcohol can blur the vision and slow the reflexes, people who have been drinking should not drive. The National Safety Council says that about half the drivers involved in accidents in which people are killed have been drinking.

One organization that has been set up to help alcoholics is called Alcoholics Anonymous, or A.A. People at an A.A. meeting discuss their drinking problems with each other. They give each other support in trying to overcome the disease. Sometimes, a drug such as Antabuse is used to help a person stop drinking. Antabuse reacts to alcohol in such a way that a person taking a drink with alcohol in it feels very uncomfortable. That person's discomfort helps him or her refuse any more alcoholic drinks. *See also* ADDICTION.

J.J.A./J.J.F.; M.H.M.

ALDEBARAN *See* STAR.

ALDER (ôl′dər) Alders are trees or bushes belonging to the birch family, Betulaceae. They have oval, toothed leaves. Most alders are found in the northern hemisphere, but a few species grow in South America. The best-known species is the black alder of Europe.

The wood of the alder, which is soft, is used in making furniture. Alders commonly grow along stream banks. They are valuable in preventing erosion and for providing food and cover for wildlife. *See also* BIRCH.

S.R.G./M.H.S.

ALEWIFE (āl′wīf′) The alewife is a silvery fish belonging to the herring family, Clupeidae. Alewives are found along the east coast of North America, from Florida to Quebec. These fish are usually anadromous. This means that they live their adult lives in the oceans but return to freshwater rivers to spawn, or lay eggs. Many die after this spawning. Alewives also live in the Great Lakes. Anadromous alewives are 10 to 12 in. [25 to 30 cm] long, while freshwater alewives are only 3 to 6 in. [8 to 15 cm] long. Both kinds have a thin body with a deeply forked tail.

Alewives are caught in nets and are used as bait, fertilizer, and pet food. They also are salted, pickled, or smoked to be eaten by people.

Alewives have not always been found in the Great Lakes. When canals were built connecting the lakes with the St. Lawrence and Hudson rivers, alewives entered the lakes and were unable to return to the sea. S.R.G./E.C.M.

ALFALFA (al fal′fə) Alfalfa, also known as lucerne, is a plant that is a member of the pea family, Leguminosae. (*See* PEA FAMILY.) It grows from 2 to 7 ft. [0.6 to 2.1 m] tall and has purple flowers. Like other legumes, alfalfa is able to absorb nitrogen from the air and put it into the soil. It is able to do this because of a bacterium that grows on its roots. Called nitrogen fixation, this process is important because nitrogen is a valuable plant nutrient that is quickly taken from the soil by other crops. Farmers plant alfalfa in fields to restore nitrogen to the soil. This helps reduce the amount of nitrogen-containing fertilizer needed.

Alfalfa is high in protein and vitamins, making it an excellent food for animals. It tolerates heat, cold, and drought. Alfalfa originally came from Asia but is now planted around the world. *See also* NITROGEN CYCLE; NITROGEN FIXATION.   S.R.G./T.L.G.; F.W.S.

ALGAE (al′jē′) Algae are simple organisms. Most algae belong to kingdom Protista. Blue-green algae belong to kingdom Monera. The illustration on page 51 shows the major algae groups. Although many of the algae are one-celled organisms, others are made up of many cells and have rootlike structures. Such algae may grow over 200 ft. [60 m] long. Algae produce food by photosynthesis. (*See* PHOTO-SYNTHESIS.) They reproduce in different ways: asexually and sexually. The one-celled algae reproduce asexually by dividing into two identical cells. Sexual reproduction involves sex cells. (*See* REPRODUCTION.)

Most algae live in the water in oceans, rivers, lakes, and ponds. Some can live in moist places on land. Algae are found on the ice in polar regions. Some are found in the hot springs at Yellowstone National Park in the western United States. These springs are nearly 187°F. [88°C]. The best-known kinds of algae are probably the seaweed found at beaches.

Algae are important because they are the beginning of some food chains that provide food for animals. Fish depend on algae for their food. People eat the fish. People also use algae directly. Many people, especially in Asia, eat certain kinds of algae, such as dulse, nori, and Irish moss. In addition, algae are used in making certain cosmetic products and such foods as ice cream, puddings, and gelatin. Diatomite, a material produced from fossilized diatom deposits, is used in such items as swimming-pool filters, insulation, and scouring powder. In sewage-treatment plants, algae

Rocky coastlines are home to many kinds of algae. The seaweed pictured provides hiding places and food for various animals.

THE MAIN GROUPS OF ALGAE AND WHERE THEY ARE FOUND

Green Algae *(Chlorophyta)*

are a varied group that commonly cause scums on ponds. Nearly all the alga forms occur. The examples shown include a single-cell *Pleurococcus*, which grows on tree trunks; a filament (series of cells arranged in a threadlike way), *Spirogyra*, which is a freshwater alga; and a multicelled flat sheet, *Ulva*, which is a seashore alga, a few inches long. Most green algae are freshwater and microscopic.

Euglenoids *(Euglenophyta)*

are single-celled forms only. They have a flagellum (taillike structure), rooted in a front pocket, and lack a cell wall, which distinguishes them from green algae. All are microscopic and very common in lakes, rivers, and ponds.

Yellow-Green Algae *(Xanthophyta)*

do not store starch in their cells, which distinguishes them from green algae. Single-celled and tube forms occur, which are mostly microscopic and freshwater.

Blue-Green Algae *(Cyanophyta)*

are more closely related to the bacteria than to other algae. There are single-celled and filament forms. They are all microscopic but can be seen as "blooms" on lakes. They have no flagella, but some can move about slowly. They are mostly freshwater.

Ulva

Pleurococcus

Ophiocytium

Nostoc

Spirogyra

Euglena

Vaucheria

Oscillatoria

Fresh water

Sea

Heterosiphonia

Laminaria

Peridinium

Coccosphaera

Eucampia

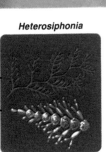

Corallina

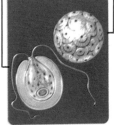

Phaeocystis

Fucus

Coscinodiscus

Ceratium

Red Seaweeds *(Rhodophyta)*

Often a foot or more in length, most red algae are many-celled and branched or blade shaped. Their sex cells, unlike those of the brown seaweed, have no flagella. They have a pigment (coloring substance) that allows them to grow at deeper levels than other algae. Most live in the sea.

Brown Seaweeds *(Phaeophyta)*

These include the largest algae—some are over 200 ft. [60 m] long. Adults are made up of millions of cells, but the sex cells are microscopic and flagellated, like the adult cells of some other algae. Most live in the sea.

Dinoflagellates *(Pyrrophyta)*

These often cause phosphorescence in seawater. All are microscopic, single-celled or colonial, with two flagella. Most live in the sea.

Golden Algae *(Chrysophyta)*

A rather mixed group of microscopic, very delicate algae. Single-celled, colonial, and filament forms are found in plankton and in cold fresh water. The very tiny Coccolithophores are marine algae covered with round chalky plates. Many chalk cliffs are made from their bodies.

Diatoms *(Bacillariophyta)*

Diatoms have hard, sculptured cell walls containing silica. All are microscopic and single-celled or colonial. They have no flagella but can move about slowly. They are common in the sea and in fresh water.

51

are used to help break down sewage into harmless chemicals.

Algae can be harmful to people when the organisms are present in great numbers. Several species of red dinoflagellates produce a poison that can paralyze a person. When a clam eats the algae, it collects this poison in its tissues. If a person then eats the clam, he or she will be poisoned. The red algae sometimes grow in large colonies. These colonies turn the water red. This is called a red tide. *See also* AGAR; DIATOM; MONERA; PROTISTA; SEAWEED. S.R.G./M.J.C.; M.H.S.

ALGEBRA (al′jə brə) is a branch of mathematics that uses symbols such as letters to stand for numbers, sets of numbers, and values of many kinds. Algebra uses equations in solving problems. The word *algebra* comes from the Arabic word *al-jebr.* The Arab mathematician al—Khowarizmi named one of his books *Al-jebr* in the ninth century. The word referred to topics dealing with equations.

One of the rules in arithmetic is $2 + 3 = 3 + 2$. A general statement taken from this example is that when any two numbers are added together in any order, the answer is the same. This same statement in algebra could be written $x + y = y + x$. The letters x and y stand for any two numbers.

For addition and subtraction in algebra, the common signs, $+$ and $-$, are used. To show that one number is to be multiplied by another, the sign x is used, or the two numbers or symbols are written next to each other. Sometimes a dot is written between the numbers or symbols. $2x$ means 2 multiplied by x (or x multiplied by 2). A simple way of showing x multiplied by x is to use an exponent. For example, xx is written as x^2. The number 2 above and to the right of the x is called the

exponent. Exponents are used to show that a number is multiplied by itself many times. 5^6 means $5 \times 5 \times 5 \times 5 \times 5 \times 5$.

Using the above rules, symbols can be combined to form algebraic expressions. The expression $x^2 + 3x - 5$ may have different values, depending on the value of x. If x equals 2, this algebraic expression can be simplified.

$$2^2 + (3 \times 2) - 5$$
$$2^2 = 2 \times 2 = 4$$
$$3 \times 2 = 6$$
$$4 + 6 - 5$$

Therefore, the expression means $4 + 6 - 5$ and the answer is 5. It makes no difference if 4 is added to 6 before or after subtracting 5. The calculation may be $10 - 5$ or $4 + 1$. The answer is still 5.

Algebraic expressions are used to solve many kinds of problems. For example, the statement "the sum of two numbers is ten" may be written $x + y = 10$. The letters x and y stand for any two numbers.

Once you have an equation, the next step is to find out when it is true. An equation is usually true only for certain values of the unknown quantity. For example, the equation $2x = 10$ is only a true statement if $x = 5$. The value of x for which the statement is true is called the solution of the equation.

To find the solutions of some equations, the equation should be thought of as a balance. Whatever is done to one side of the equation must be done to the other side. To solve the equation $2x + 3 = 7$, the diagram

shows the $2x + 3$ in the left-hand pan balanced by the 7 in the right-hand pan.

Subtracting 3 from both sides of the equation, the equation becomes $2x = 4$. The pans still balance.

Dividing both sides of the equation by 2, the equation becomes $x = 2$. The solution of the equation is $x = 2$.

More difficult problems are written as equations with two unknown quantities. For instance, an equation might need two numbers that add up to 10. If the two numbers are written as x and y, we can write the expression as $x + y = 10$. If $x = y$, then there is only one solution: x and y must each equal 5. If $x \neq y$, some solutions for $x + y = 10$ could be $x = 1$, $y = 9$; or $x = 2$, $y = 8$; or $x = 3$, $y = 7$. This type of equation is called indeterminate.

Another equation might be $x - y = 2$. This equation has many possible solutions, such as $x = 4$, $y = 2$; or $x = 7$, $y = 5$; and so on. If the equations $x + y = 10$ and $x - y = 2$ are put together, there is only one set of values of x and y that can satisfy both of them. The solution is $x = 6$ and $y = 4$.

Using a graph is one way to find the solution. The values of x are shown on the numbered line going from left to right across the page. This is called the x-axis. The values of y go up and down on the other numbered line.

This is the y-axis. Some of the solutions of the equation $x + y = 10$ are

$$x = 0, y = 10$$
$$x = 2, y = 8$$
$$x = 4, y = 6.$$

These solutions are marked by the points in red. For example, the point showing the solution $x = 4$, $y = 6$, is found by moving 4 units across the x-axis and 6 units up the y-axis.

Some solutions of the equation $x - y = 2$ are:

$$x = 10, y = 8$$
$$x = 8, y = 6$$
$$x = 6, y = 4.$$

These solutions are marked by the green points. By connecting the two sets of points, you get two straight lines. These lines are the graphs of the two equations. The point at which the lines cross marks the solution of both equations $x + y = 10$ and $x - y = 2$.

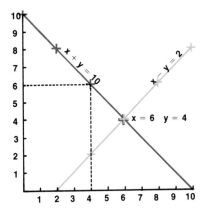

Mathematics includes many different kinds of algebra to solve problems. Algebra experts are concerned with different symbols and the rules for using them. Algebra has been used to solve problems in chemistry, physics, and engineering. J.J.A./S.P.A.; R.J.S.

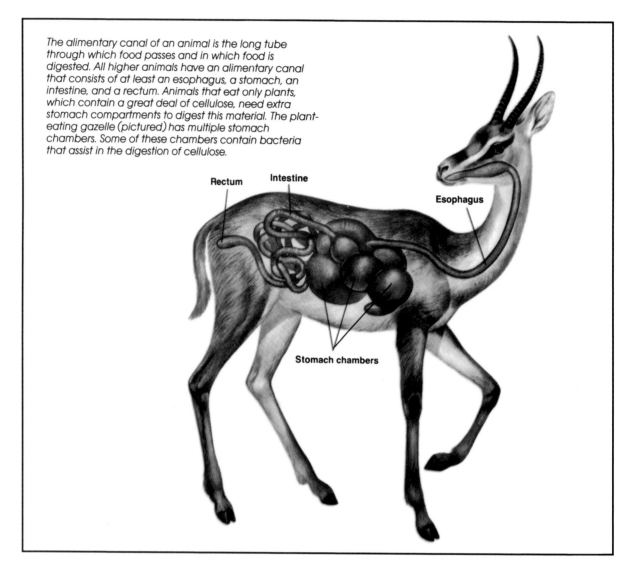

The alimentary canal of an animal is the long tube through which food passes and in which food is digested. All higher animals have an alimentary canal that consists of at least an esophagus, a stomach, an intestine, and a rectum. Animals that eat only plants, which contain a great deal of cellulose, need extra stomach compartments to digest this material. The plant-eating gazelle (pictured) has multiple stomach chambers. Some of these chambers contain bacteria that assist in the digestion of cellulose.

Rectum

Intestine

Esophagus

Stomach chambers

ALIMENTARY CANAL The alimentary (al′ə ment′ə rē) canal is also called the digestive or gastrointestinal tract. It is a long tube within the body of an animal. It usually begins at the mouth and ends at the anus. Some simple animals, such as the Cnidarians, have only one opening.

Food passes through the alimentary canal to be digested and absorbed into the body tissues. Undigested food and wastes are expelled through the anus. *See also* ANUS; DIGESTION; ESOPHAGUS; INTESTINE; STOMACH.

S.R.B./J.J.F.; L.O.S.

ALKALI (al′kə lī′) An alkali is a base that dissolves easily in water. A solution of a strong alkali has a soapy feeling and a bitter taste. The solution can corrode other substances. It must be handled carefully.

Using an indicator is one way of telling whether a solution is alkaline. Red litmus paper will turn blue in an alkali solution.

If an acid and an alkali are mixed in water, a salt is formed. When dry, solid acids and dry alkalis are mixed, no neutralizing chemical change occurs. Ordinary baking powder is a mixture of dry acid and dry, alkaline salt.

MIXING ALKALI AND ACID

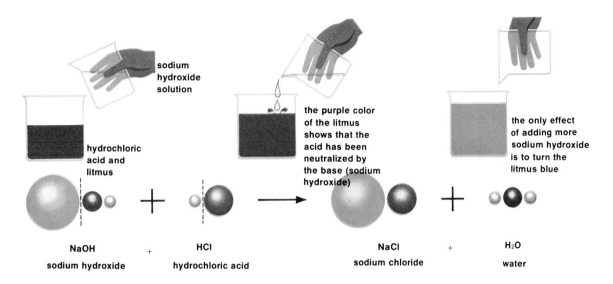

sodium hydroxide solution

hydrochloric acid and litmus

the purple color of the litmus shows that the acid has been neutralized by the base (sodium hydroxide)

the only effect of adding more sodium hydroxide is to turn the litmus blue

NaOH + HCl → NaCl + H₂O
sodium hydroxide   hydrochloric acid   sodium chloride   water

This diagram shows what happens when an alkali and acid interact chemically. Sodium hydroxide is a strong alkali. When a water solution of sodium hydroxide is mixed with hydrochloric acid, a neutral salt, sodium chloride, is formed. The litmus indicator is red in acid and blue in alkali.

Strong alkalis are used as cleaning substances. They are also used in the making of soap. The best known strong alkalis are sodium hydroxide (NaOH), also called caustic soda, and potassium hydroxide (KOH), known as caustic potash. Potassium hydroxide is used mainly in the making of soap and in medicine. Sodium hydroxide is used in the manufacture of other chemicals, rayon, film, and soap. It is also used in medicine. *See also* ACID; BASE.   J.J.A./A.D.

ALKALI METAL The alkali (al′kə lī′) metals are a group of six elements: lithium (Li), sodium (Na), potassium (K), rubidium (Rb), cesium (Cs), and francium (Fr). These metals are not found in nature. They are found only as ions in different chemicals. (*See* IONS AND IONIZATION.)

Each of the alkali metals has a silvery shine. Each is a good conductor of electricity and heat. Each is easily molded or shaped.

These metals are soft. They can be cut with a knife. The alkali metals are difficult to handle and store because of their chemical reactivity. They are often stored under kerosene or some other liquid. They react violently with water, giving off hydrogen and forming bases. All the alkali metals have a valence of one. This means that they gain or share one electron in bonding with other atoms. *See also* ALKALI; BASE; ELEMENT; VALENCE.

J.J.A./A.D.

ALKALINE EARTH METAL The alkaline (al′kə lən) earth metals are a group of six elements: beryllium (Be), magnesium (Mg), calcium (Ca), strontium (Sr), barium (Ba), and radium (Ra). They are usually found in the earth. The alkaline earth metals are harder and have higher melting points and boiling points than the alkali metals have. (*See* ALKALI METAL.) The alkaline earth metals react with water, giving off hydrogen gas and form-

55

ing bases. They do not react as rapidly as the alkali metals.

All the alkaline earth metals gain or share two electrons in bonding with other atoms, giving them a valence of two. This means that they gain or share two electrons in bonding with other atoms. *See also* ALKALI; BASE; ELEMENT; VALENCE.   J.J.A./A.D.

ALKALOID (al′kə lȯid′) An alkaloid is an organic compound containing nitrogen (N). Alkaloids are made by plants as waste products. They serve no useful purpose for the plants. Alkaloids are solids that appear as crystals, except for coniine, found in hemlock, and nicotine, found in tobacco. Both of these alkaloids are liquids. Alkaloids dissolve in alcohol, but not in water. Alkaloids often have harsh effects on animals, including humans.

Some alkaloids, such as coniine, are deadly poisons. Strychnine, which comes from various trees, causes muscles to shake and tighten. Curare, a mixture of alkaloids, also comes from trees. Curare was first used by natives in South America. They dipped their arrowheads in it so that animals died when wounded. Also known as arrow poison, curare relaxes muscles. It is sometimes used in surgery for this purpose.

Alkaloids have been used to kill insects. Small doses of belladonna were once used by women to improve their beauty. The drug makes the pupils of the eyes larger. Morphine, from the opium poppy, and cocaine, from the coca plant, were once widely used as anesthetics. They are now seldom used for this purpose because they are addictive. Quinine, from the bark of cinchona, was used to fight the disease malaria. Caffeine is an alkaloid in coffee, tea, and other substances. Theobromine occurs in cocoa.   J.J.A./J.M.

ALLERGY (al′ər jē) An allergy is an abnormal sensitivity of the body to certain substances. For most people, these substances are harmless. Some things to which a person may be allergic are feathers, dust, pollen from plants, certain foods, some medicines, and bee stings. Substances to which people are allergic are called allergens. One person may be allergic to feathers, but another person may not be. Feathers are an allergen only to the first person.

Many people are allergic to poison ivy. Contact with the plant can cause reddening, itching, and blistering of the skin.

When an allergic person comes near an allergen, he or she may react by sneezing, coughing, or even vomiting. His or her eyes may tear or redden. The person may break out in a rash or hives, which are spots of fluid in the skin. Some people have very serious allergic reactions in which they have trouble breathing. Some allergic reactions last for a few hours. Some last several days. Several common disorders, partly or wholly caused by allergens, are asthma, eczema, and hay fever. Sensitivity to allergens may be inherited.

During an allergic reaction, several parts of the body's immune system are activated by and help attack the allergen. Immune cells called lymphocytes produce large numbers of proteins called antibodies. Antibodies combine with the allergen to cause the release of certain substances from the body cells into the blood and other body fluids. These substances, called H-substances, bring about various reactions. These reactions include attracting additional immune cells (more lymphocytes as well as other cells), causing blood vessels to dilate (widen), and causing fluid to build up in the area. Some of the lymphocytes attack the allergen directly, without making antibodies. The result of all these actions is the so-called inflammatory response, which is responsible for the symptoms—such as sneezing or rash—mentioned above.

The main H-substance is called histamine. Antihistamines are drugs that reduce the effects of histamines. For example, antihistamines can reduce sneezing and help control the itching of a rash.

Some people have antibodies that react to penicillin, a drug that is helpful to most people. The reaction to a dose of penicillin may be fatal to a person with an allergy to it. Such a reaction is called anaphylactic shock. *See also* ANTIBODY; ASTHMA; ECZEMA; IMMUNITY.

S.R.G./J.J.F.; M.H.M.; J.E.P.

ALLIGATOR (al′ə gāt′ər) Alligators are reptiles that are related to crocodiles. (*See* CROCODILE.) The largest species is the American alligator, which grows to 19 ft. [5.7 m] long. It is found only in the southeastern United States. A smaller species, the Chinese alligator, grows to 6 ft. [1.8 m] long and is found along the Chang (Yangtse) River in China. All species of alligators live in warm climates.

Alligators live near water where they eat fish, frogs, birds, and other animals. Very large adults can eat a deer, or, very rarely, a human. Alligators have large mouths and many sharp teeth. They make nests at the edge of water and lay twenty to fifty eggs during the summer.

Alligators, such as this one photographed in the Everglades National Park in Florida, are the largest reptiles in North America. Some alligators grow to a length of 19 ft. (5.7 m).

Alligator meat has become increasingly popular for human consumption, especially in such states as Louisiana and Florida. The meat comes primarily from the alligator's tail.

Alligators are very similar to crocodiles. Crocodiles have pointed noses, however. Alligators have blunt noses. *See also* CAIMAN; REPTILE.   S.R.G./C.J.C.; T.L.G.

ALLOY (al'òi') Most alloys are a mixture of two or more metals. The metals are combined by heating them until they become liquid. An alloy is made when the metals remain evenly mixed after cooling and becoming solid.

Metals in their pure form are often too weak for most uses. They can be improved by mixing one or more other metals with them to form alloys. For example, pure aluminum is light, but weak. When copper and magnesium are added to it, the aluminum becomes stronger. Copper and tin are soft and weak. Mixed together in an alloy, they form the harder, stronger bronze. Brass, a mixture of copper and zinc, is another strong and useful alloy. Copper is often used in making alloys. It is used in cupronickel, from which some coins are made.

Alloys can also be made by adding a nonmetal, such as carbon or silicon, to a metal. Steel is made of carbon, iron, and traces of other metals. Iron by itself is very weak and soft compared with steel. Only a small amount of carbon is needed to make the change to steel. Ordinary steel contains less than 0.25 percent carbon.

Alloys do more than just make a metal harder and stronger. Each type of element mixed has a certain effect on the total mass of metal. If chromium, nickel, and molybdenum are added to steel, the rust-free alloy called stainless steel is produced. Stainless steel, also

stronger than ordinary steel, is only one of many alloy steels used in industry.

Pewter is an alloy made of lead, antimony, and copper. Pewter has been used for dishes, flatware, and other utensils for centuries.

Most metals dissolve in one another in certain proportions. However, copper and nickel can mix together, no matter how much of either element is used. They are said to be totally miscible. A few pairs of metals, such as lead and aluminum, are immiscible. They cannot be mixed together at all.

Alloys usually have cooling rates different from those of pure metals. Pure metals turn solid at a specific temperature. Above that temperature, they are liquid. Below it, they are solid. Most alloys have a range. This means an alloy may turn solid anywhere between many degrees of temperature. An equal mixture of the copper-nickel alloy, for instance, has a range from 2,394°F. [1,312°C] to 2,278°F. [1,248°C].

A few alloys behave like pure metals, melting at certain temperatures. In all these alloys, the amount of each metal used is such that the lowest possible melting point is obtained. Wood's metal is one example. An alloy of bismuth, lead, tin, and cadmium, it melts at 158°F. [70°C]. It is used in valves of

SOME IMPORTANT ALLOYS

Ferrous alloys (mainly iron)	Major Properties	Major Uses	Typical amounts of elements other than iron
High-alloy steels and stainless steels	Very hard, strong steels, often resistant to corrosion.	Tools to cut and drill other metals, and high-strength metal parts. Stainless steels are often used for cutlery.	0.1-2.0% carbon, up to 27% chromium or 20% tungsten or 15% nickel, and lesser amounts of vanadium, cobalt, molybdenum, zirconium, or tantalum.
Mild steels	Hard, strong, workable steels, more resistant to corrosion than pure iron.	Steel constructions other than those above. Widely used for automobiles and ships.	0.1-1.5% carbon, very small amounts of other elements.
Cast iron	Hard but brittle.	Widely used in early industrial times.	2-3% carbon, a few percent silicon and other elements.

Nonferrous alloys (little or no iron)	Major Properties	Major Uses	Typical amounts of elements
Aluminum alloys	Fairly hard and strong, very light alloys, often with good corrosion resistance and good electrical conductivity.	Tubes for boilers, automobile bodies, buildings, food equipment, foil kitchenware, electric cables, nuts, bolts, ships' tubes and sheets. Widely used when lightness plus strength is required.	77.5% copper, 2% aluminum, 20.5% zinc.
Aluminum bronze	Tough, but workable, and resistant to corrosion by seawater.	Nuts, bolts, ships' tubes and sheets.	77.5% copper, 2% aluminum, 20.5% zinc.
Manganese bronze	Very good resistance to wear.	Automobile clutch disks, valves.	58.5% copper, 39% zinc, 1.5% iron, 1.0% tin.
Phosphor bronze	Strong, fairly corrosion resistant, good electrical conductivity.	Chemical equipment, electric motor brushes.	95% copper, 5% tin.
Bronze	Resistant to corrosion by seawater.	Superstructure and other parts on ships.	90% copper, 10% zinc.
Naval brass	Fairly strong and workable. Attractive yellow color.	Portholes and other parts on ships.	60% copper, 39% zinc, 1% tin.
Red brass	Workable, fairly resistant to corrosion.	Plumbing for houses (but plastics often replace it).	85% copper, 15% zinc.
Copper-nickel alloys	Hard, heat and corrosion resistant.	Chemical equipment.	69-88.5% copper, 10-30% nickel, some iron and manganese.
Nickel-copper alloys	Hard, resistant to many acids and bases.	Chemical equipment.	About 31% copper, 64% nickel, small amounts of carbon, iron, manganese, and silicon.
Nickel-chromium alloys	Very resistant to heat. Good resistance to corrosion.	Airplane exhausts, food and dairy equipment.	About 68% nickel, 15% chromium, 9% iron, small amounts of carbon, copper, manganese, silicon, and tellurium.
Nickel-molybdenum alloys	Extremely good heat resistance. Good resistance to corrosion.	Jet airplane engines, missiles, furnaces.	About 55% nickel, 30% molybdenum, 5% zinc, 4% iron, 2.5% copper, some carbon, chromium, manganese, silicon, and silver.
Lead alloys	Soft, but antimony lead is harder. Good acid resistance (not oxidizing acids).	House roofs and acid equipment. Antimony lead is used for storage battery grids.	94-99.7% lead, up to 6% antimony.
Pewter	Attractive shiny gray color.	Drinking mugs and ornamental objects.	91% lead, 7% antimony, 2% copper.
White metal	A fairly soft alloy.	Bearings for motors.	92% tin, 8% antimony.
Magnesium alloys	Very light, fairly hard. Not very resistant to corrosion.	Small parts for engines, where lightness is very important.	About 90% magnesium, 7% aluminum, 1.5% zinc, and some manganese.
*Titanium alloys	Lightweight, very strong, resistant to corrosion.	Jet airplane, missile, and ship engines, and chemical equipment.	Mostly titanium, with up to 13% vanadium, 11% chromium, 8% manganese, 6% aluminum, and some other metals.
Noble metal alloys	Generally rather soft and workable. Resist corrosion well. Often very heat resistant.	Expensive alloys used in jewelry. Harder types, such as osmiridium, are used in fountain pen tips.	Alloys containing platinum, rhodium, osmium, iridium, ruthenium, palladium, and gold or silver.

* Although used only recently, titanium is the ninth most common element in the earth's crust.

sprinkler systems in public buildings. There, if a fire starts, its heat melts the Wood's metal seal. This releases the water to put out the fire. Such alloys, and their melting temperatures, are called eutectic.   J.J.A./A.D.

ALLUVIUM (ə lü′vē əm) Alluvium is gravel, sand, silt, or mud that has been deposited by water. Alluvium is found at the banks and mouths of rivers or alongside lakes and oceans. It is also found where rivers, lakes, or oceans once existed but have since dried up.

Erosion washes soil into streams. The streams carry the soil downstream. When the speed of the water slows, the water cannot carry the heavier objects that are in it. These objects are dropped and left behind. Also, when a stream enters a larger stream or body of water such as a lake, it will drop its load of soil. Gravel is deposited first because it is the heaviest. Silt and mud are light. They remain suspended in the water until the stream that carries them reaches the mouth of the river. Deltas are alluvial deposits, usually consisting of silt and mud, found at the mouths of some rivers. Alluvial plains are found in flat valleys where the river has flooded and deposited mud. Alluvial plains are among the most fertile and densely populated regions in the world. *See also* SOIL.   S.R.G./W.R.S.

ALMOND (äl′mənd) The almond tree belongs to the rose family, Rosaceae. Its nutlike fruit is called an almond. The almond is not really a nut. It is a hard seed from a fleshy fruit similar to a peach. The tree is small, only growing to 20 ft. [6 m]. It is very attractive. It resembles the peach tree, to which it is related. The almond tree is originally from southwest Asia. It now grows in warm climates around the world. In the United States, almonds are grown in California.

Alluvium that has been deposited along the shore of the Potomac River in Virginia is pictured at left. Alluvium consists of gravel, sand, silt, or mud.

There are two types of almonds. One is bitter, and one is sweet. The sweet almond is eaten and used in foods. The bitter almond contains small amounts of the deadly poison, hydrocyanic acid.   S.R.G./F.W.S.

ALOE (al′ō′) The aloes are a group of succulent plants belonging to the lily family, Liliaceae. (*See* LILY FAMILY.) They grow rosettes, which are spiral-shaped bunches of fleshy leaves. A tall spike of flowers grows up from

Aloe plants are members of the lily family. Their fleshy leaves grow in spiral-shaped bunches.

the center. Aloes are found in the dry regions of Africa and Asia. They are similar to the agaves of the Americas. (*See* AGAVE.) Aloes are grown for decoration and are used in medicine.   S.R.G./M.H.S.

ALPHA CENTAURI (al′fə sen tȯr′ī) Alpha Centauri is the name of the star system that is closest to earth and that is the third brightest in the sky. Alpha Centauri is a member of the constellation Centaurus. This constellation is in the southern hemisphere of the sky. Alpha Centauri is about 4.3 light-years away from earth. Traveling at the speed of light (186,282 mi. per second or 299,792 km per second), it would take an object four years and three

months to get to Alpha Centauri from earth. Scientists once believed that Alpha Centauri was a single star. It is now known that it is a triple star. One of its stars, Proxima Centauri, is the nearest star to our sun. *See also* ASTRONOMY; CONSTELLATION; STAR.   G.M.B./D.H.M.; C.R.

ALPHA CRUCIS *See* STAR.

ALPHA PARTICLE (al′fə pärt′i kəl) Alpha particles are positively charged particles given off by the nuclei of certain radioactive atoms. (*See* RADIOACTIVITY.) Alpha particles are made up of two neutrons and two protons bound together. Alpha particles are identical to the nuclei of helium atoms. They were discovered by Ernest Rutherford in 1899. (*See* ATOM; RUTHERFORD, ERNEST.)

Radioactive elements such as uranium and radium give off alpha and beta particles and gamma rays. Alpha particles are the least dangerous of the three because they can be stopped by a piece of paper or by a few centimeters of air. Alpha particles are not harmful to humans unless they actually enter the body.

Alpha particles can be detected by a Geiger counter. They will also leave tracks on photographic film or make a flash of light on a fluorescent screen. *See also* BETA PARTICLE; GAMMA RAY; GEIGER COUNTER. W.R.P./J.T.; E.D.W.

ALTAIR *See* STAR.

ALTERNATING CURRENT An alternating current is an electrical current that changes direction regularly. It can be produced by an electrical generator. (*See* GENERATOR, ELECTRICAL.) A generator has a coil of wire spinning between the poles of a magnet. The magnet causes a current to flow in the coil as it spins. The direction of the current changes twice in every spin. During the first quarter of the spin, the current builds up to a maximum in one direction. Then it goes back to zero at the end of half of the spin. At this point, the current changes direction. It then builds up to a maximum in the other direction and reduces to zero after it has completed the spin. This is called a cycle. Usually there is a complete cycle every fraction of a second. When the coil spins around once, the current goes through one complete cycle. At the end of the cycle, the current changes direction to start a new cycle. This is the most common way of producing an alternating current. Another way is to spin the magnet around inside the coil of wire. *See also* ELECTROMAGNETISM.

M.E./J.T.

ALTERNATION OF GENERATIONS Alternation of generations is the alternation of two distinct stages in an organism's life cycle. It is characteristic of some lower animals, such as some members of the phyla Platyhelminthes and Cnidaria, as well as some protozoans. Also, many plants—and algae and fungi—experience alternation of generations.

In alternation of generations, the gametophyte (gamete-producing) generation alternates with the sporophyte (spore-producing) generation. The gametophyte, or haploid, generation is the sexually reproductive stage in an organism's life cycle. It produces male gametes (sperm) and female gametes (eggs), which combine to form a zygote. (*See* GAMETE; ZYGOTE.) The zygote develops into a new organism, the sporophyte. The sporophyte, or diploid, generation is the asexually reproductive stage in an organism's life cycle. The sporophyte produces spores, which develop into new organisms. (*See* SPORE.)

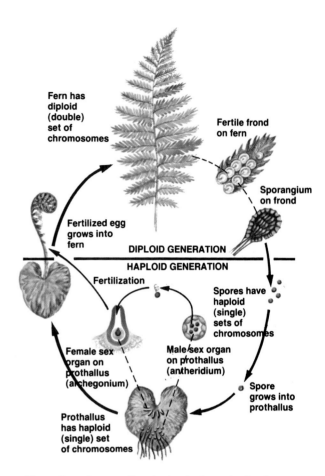

Alternation of generations is clearly shown by the fern plant. The fern (top) is the diploid generation, having a double set of chromosomes. The smaller prothallus plant (bottom) is the haploid generation, having a single set of chromosomes.

Although alternation of generations is common in many organisms, one of the two stages may be difficult to observe. This may be due to the fact that it is very small or short-lived. Frequently, one generation looks totally different from the other generation, even though the same species is involved. *See also* ASEXUAL REPRODUCTION; REPRODUCTION; SEX.

A.J.C./M.J.C.; E.R.L.

ALTIMETER (al tim′ət ər) An altimeter is an instrument in an airplane that shows how high the plane is above the earth. The barometric or aneroid altimeter, used in many small planes, shows the height above sea level. It measures the decrease in air pressure as the altitude increases. Because air pressure on the ground varies as part of the changing weather, this type of altimeter must be adjusted to the air pressure on the ground before each flight.

Most large planes carry altimeters that are more accurate than the barometric type. Radio or absolute altimeters bounce electronic signals off the earth's surface, much like radar. The time it takes for the echoes to return is interpreted into a precise measurement of the altitude. The capacitance altimeter indicates altitude by measuring the difference between electrical charges of the earth and the airplane. The sonic altimeter bounces sound signals off the earth's surface. It times the echoes to determine the altitude. *See also* ATMOSPHERE; BAROMETER. W.R.P./R.W.L.

ALTITUDE (al′tə tüd′) Altitude is the height of an object above a given level. For example, the altitude of an airplane in flight is measured from the ground. The altitude of a geographical feature such as a mountain is measured from the surface of the ocean (sea level). The altitude of the sun, moon, stars, and planets is measured from the earth's horizon and is given as an angle in degrees, minutes, and seconds.

Airplanes carry instruments called altimeters that measure in feet or meters the altitudes at which an airplane flies. (*See* ALTIMETER.) The altitudes of mountains are called elevations. Mt. Everest, the highest mountain on earth, has an elevation of 29,028 ft. [8,848 m]. Many maps show altitudes of land with contour lines. W.R.P./J.VP.

ALUM (al′əm) Alum is the name for any of a group of hydrated (water-containing) double salts. One common alum is potassium alumi-

num sulfate, also called potash alum. It forms colorless eight-sided crystals, known as octahedrons. Alum is produced by evaporation of a water solution that contains aluminum sulfate and potassium sulfate, and its chemical formula is $KAl(SO_4)_2 \cdot 12H_2O$. Potash alum is used in dyeing leather, paper, and fabrics. It is also used in medicine to stop small cuts from bleeding. Alums are also used to purify water. Most alums are manufactured from the ore known as bauxite. *See also* BAUXITE; HYDRATE; SALTS; SULFATE. J.J.A./A.D.; E.W.L.

ALUMINUM (ə lü′mə nəm) Aluminum is a silvery white metallic element with the symbol Al. It was discovered by Friedrich Wohler, a German chemist, in 1827. Aluminum is the most abundant metal in the earth's crust, making up 8 percent of the crust. However, for many years, producing aluminum was an expensive process. Then, in 1886, an inexpensive way of producing pure aluminum was developed. It is now a widely used metal. The atomic number of aluminum is 13, and its atomic weight is 26.98. It melts at 1,220°F. [660°C] and boils at 4,472°F. [2,467°C].

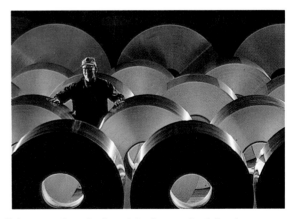

This processing plant contains large rolls of sheet aluminum. One of the main uses of aluminum is in the production of cans that hold a variety of products.

Extraction Most aluminum comes from a mineral called bauxite. (*See* BAUXITE.) Bauxite

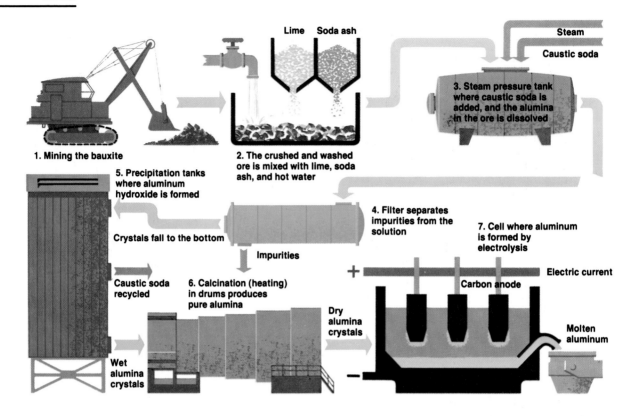

Lime   Soda ash

Steam

Caustic soda

3. Steam pressure tank where caustic soda is added, and the alumina in the ore is dissolved

1. Mining the bauxite

2. The crushed and washed ore is mixed with lime, soda ash, and hot water

5. Precipitation tanks where aluminum hydroxide is formed

Crystals fall to the bottom

4. Filter separates impurities from the solution

7. Cell where aluminum is formed by electrolysis

Electric current

Carbon anode

Impurities

Caustic soda recycled

6. Calcination (heating) in drums produces pure alumina

Dry alumina crystals

+

Molten aluminum

Wet alumina crystals

−

contains aluminum oxide, often called alumina. The alumina is obtained from the bauxite by washing and refining. Then it is mixed with cryolite, another mineral that contains aluminum. A powerful electric current is passed through the mixture in an electrolytic cell. (*See* ELECTROLYSIS.) The current generates a temperature of about 1,832°F. [1,000°C]. The aluminum melts and falls to the bottom of the cell, where it is collected. This process requires large amounts of electricity. About 10 kilowatt hours of electricity are needed to make 1 lb. [0.5 kg] of aluminum. Because of this, most aluminum is extracted in areas where hydroelectric power is plentiful and therefore inexpensive.

Uses of aluminum Aluminum is a very light, yet strong, metal with many different uses. It is used for making pots and pans because it is a good conductor of heat. Aluminum also conducts electricity well and is used to make electrical wires. Aluminum is used to make cans for various beverages and other liquids. It can be pressed into a thin foil that is used both commercially and in homes for such purposes as wrapping foods for storage.

Because aluminum is light but strong, it is widely used in airplanes and spacecraft. It can be made even stronger by mixing it with other metals to form alloys. (*See* ALLOY.) Duralumin is such an alloy. It is used as the outer surface of many airplanes. The bodies and parts of some automobiles, trucks, boats, and trains are made from aluminum alloys.

Seawater corrodes pure aluminum. (*See* CORROSION.) Alloys of aluminum have been developed that do not corrode. Aluminum is not corroded by fresh water or by the atmosphere. This is because aluminum forms a thin coating of its oxide on its surface. This is called anodizing. Manufacturers anodize such products as window frames, screen doors, and drainpipes. *See also* ANODIZING; OXIDE.

M.E./J.R.W.

ALVAREZ, LUIS (1911-1988) Luis Alvarez was an American physicist and Nobel-prize winner. Alvarez is best known for his discoveries of atomic particles in the 1950s and 1960s. Alvarez discovered these particles using a device he invented, called a bubble chamber. (*See* ACCELERATORS, PARTICLE.)

Luis Alvarez (left) and his son Walter Alvarez

Alvarez was born in San Francisco, California. He entered the University of Chicago, where he studied physics, in 1929. While in Chicago, he met the physicist Ernest Lawrence. (*See* LAWRENCE, ERNEST.) Lawrence invited Alvarez to work at the Lawrence Radiation Laboratory at the University of California at Berkeley. There, Alvarez worked with other scientists using a device called a cyclotron to study atoms. A cyclotron is a particle accelerator shaped in a circle. In World War II (1939-1945), Alvarez directed the development of a radar system called Ground-Controlled Approach (GCA). GCA uses radio waves to guide planes through fog or darkness to a safe landing. (*See* RADAR.)

Alvarez also worked on the development of the atomic bomb. When the atomic bomb was dropped on Hiroshima, Japan, in 1945, Alvarez flew in a plane that accompanied the bomber. He measured the blast of the bomb using instruments he had designed and built. (*See* NUCLEAR WEAPONS.)

Alvarez and his son Walter also are known for their theory about the extinction of the dinosaurs. Their theory says that a large body from space crashed into the earth about 65 million years ago. The smoke and dust from the crash blocked the sun's light. Without sunlight, plants died. The animals that fed on the plants, including the dinosaurs, starved and froze to death. *See also* DINOSAUR.

C.C./L.W.

ALVAREZ, WALTER *See* ALVAREZ, LUIS.

ALZHEIMER'S DISEASE (älts′hī mərz diz-ēz′) Alzheimer's disease is a disorder affecting certain parts of the brain. It causes a weakening of the mind and body, including the immune system. (*See* IMMUNITY.) Alzheimer's disease usually affects elderly people. Only a small number of people have Alzheimer's disease before age sixty-five.

Symptoms of Alzheimer's disease include memory loss; difficulty learning and remembering new information; and difficulty speaking and coordinating muscles. As the disease progresses, the symptoms worsen. An Alzheimer's victim may forget how to eat, use the toilet, or bathe. As the victim's body becomes weaker, so does his or her immune system. Usually, death results from infection.

In 1990, scientists determined that Alzheimer's disease is caused by a gene that is abnormal. However, scientists do not yet know the exact location of the gene on the chromosome. (*See* CHROMOSOME; GENE.) Once the location is known, scientists would then only need to develop a blood test to determine whether a person has the disease. This test would most likely predict the presence of the disease long before its symptoms appear. By further studying the gene, scientists hope to develop treatments to cure or even prevent Alzheimer's disease. Today, doctors use medical tests involving radiation to help diagnose Alzheimer's disease in its early stages. These tests show a slowing of activity in certain parts of the brain. Early diagnosis can help the patient and family cope with the symptoms. For example, the patient and family can receive help from support groups. *See also* BRAIN. C.C.; P.W./J.E.P

AM *See* RADIO.

AMALGAM (ə mal′gəm) An amalgam is an alloy of a metal with mercury. (*See* ALLOY.) Mercury is normally a liquid, and so an amalgam is often a liquid. An amalgam may also be a solid, depending on how much metal is used in relation to the amount of mercury.

Precious metals, such as gold and silver, can be dissolved out of their ores with the use of mercury. The gold or silver is then removed from the amalgam by boiling off the mercury. Dentists use silver and other amalgams for the fillings they put in teeth. Some dentists believe that such fillings may result in a harmful accumulation of mercury in a person's body. There is disagreement over this issue. *See also* MERCURY. J.J.A./A.D.; E.W.L.

AMARANTH FAMILY About five hundred species of herbaceous, dicotyledon plants make up the amaranth (am′ə ranth′) family, Amaranthaceae. (*See* DICOTYLEDON; HERBACEOUS PLANT.) These plants are found in warm regions, including in the southern and southwestern United States. Many of the plants are considered troublesome weeds, such as the tumbleweed. Others have long-lasting green or red flowers, such as the popular garden plant called love-lies-bleeding. One variety of amaranth was cultivated as a grain by the ancient Aztecs of Mexico. It has recently become recognized again as a food crop. Its seeds have higher-quality protein than wheat. Researchers hope to develop new amaranth grains that give high yields even in harsh climates or difficult soils.

C.C.; S.R.G./M.H.S.

AMARYLLIS FAMILY There are more than 1,300 species of monocotyledons in the amaryllis (am′ə ril′əs) family, Amaryllidaceae. (*See* MONOCOTYLEDON.) These plants closely resemble members of the lily family. (*See* LILY FAMILY.) Most amaryllis species are tropical

Daffodils are members of the amaryllis family.

or subtropical. Many grow in dry regions. There are about forty species in North America, including the daffodil and snowdrop. The plants in this family have long stems; numerous narrow leaves; and large, sweet-smelling flowers.

S.R.G./M.H.S.

AMBER (am′bər) Amber is pine tree sap that dripped out of the trees millions of years ago and was buried. During the time it was buried, it hardened into a yellow or brown stone that looks like glass. Sometimes, insects fell into the sticky sap, which is also called resin. They became fossils inside the amber. Amber is now used for many things, including beads, combs, and umbrella handles. S.R.G./W.R.S.

AMEBA (ə mē′bə) An ameba is an organism having only one cell. It is a protozoan in the kingdom Protista. (*See* PROTOZOA.) Most amebas can be seen only with a microscope. They live in water or in places that are moist, such as under wet leaves. The ameba is one of the most common organisms on earth. Amebas can even be found inside the intestinal

tracts of human beings and other animals. Some species of amebas cause disease.

Everything the ameba needs is in its one cell. Its nucleus acts as its control center, and its vacuoles store foods and waste. The ameba's cell is filled with a substance called cytoplasm, as are the cells in the human body. (*See* CELL; CYTOPLASM; VACUOLE.)

An ameba feeds on bacteria. Its soft body wraps around a bacterium (singular of *bacteria*) and surrounds it. The bacterium is then enclosed in a food vacuole and digested. The ameba moves by slowly projecting a part of its body forward and letting the rest of its body ooze up to it. The part of the body projected is called a *pseudopodium*, which means "false foot." The ameba reproduces by cell division to form two identical cells. *See also* REPRODUCTION. S.R.G./M.J.C.; C.S.H.

AMERICIUM *See* ELEMENT.

AMETHYST (am′ə thəst) Amethyst is a variety of quartz, found in the form of six-sided, pointed crystals. These bluish violet or purple crystals are frequently found in lumps of rock

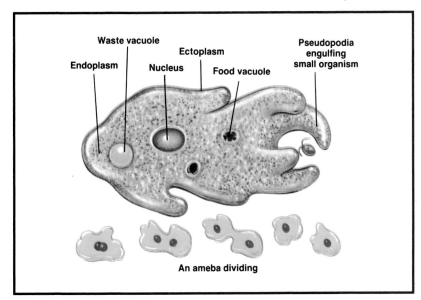

Waste vacuole
Ectoplasm
Pseudopodia engulfing small organism
Endoplasm
Nucleus
Food vacuole

An ameba dividing

Amebas feed by engulfing their food and then bringing it into their bodies. Amebas reproduce by simple fission. The nucleus divides, splitting the cell in two.

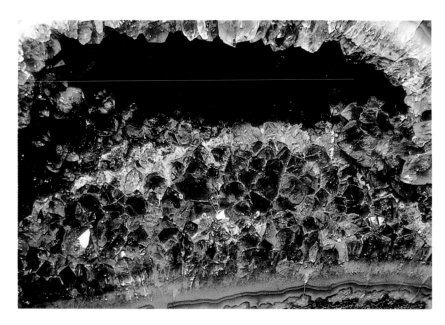

Amethyst is a form of quartz. Its beautiful purple color makes it a popular semiprecious stone.

called geodes. Amethyst has a hardness of 7 on Mohs scale. (*See* CRYSTAL; GEODE; HARDNESS; QUARTZ.) When heated, amethyst turns to a brilliant yellow or a light brown.

Amethyst is used in jewelry. It is the birthstone for February. The most prized amethysts are transparent, with a deep, even color. The color is caused by iron and manganese oxides. (*See* OXIDE.) Oriental amethyst, the same bluish violet or purple color as true amethyst, is a form of corundum. *See also* CORUNDUM.

J.J.A./R.H.; E.W.L.

AMINE (ə mēn′) An amine is a chemical compound. It is a base that reacts with an acid to form a salt. It is usually formed from ammonia (NH_3). (*See* AMMONIA.) To form amines, the hydrogen atoms in ammonia are replaced with radicals containing carbon atoms. (*See* RADICAL.) If an amine contains one of these carbon radicals, it is called a primary amine. If it contains two of the radicals, it is called a secondary amine. Most amines have a fishy or musty smell. They are used in making dyes.

S.R.G./J.M.

AMINO ACID (ə mē′nō′ as′əd) An amino acid is an organic (carbon-containing) compound possessing both acidic and basic characteristics. (*See* ACID; BASE.) Most amino acids have the following general chemical structure:

$$R \equiv C - COOH$$

with NH_2 above and H below the C.

NH_2 is called the amino group, COOH is the carboxyl acid group, and R represents the rest of the molecule. The differences in R make one amino acid different from another.

Amino acids are the building blocks of proteins. (*See* PROTEIN.) Proteins are made of long, complex chains of amino acids. These chains contain as few as four or as many as several hundred amino acids. Most proteins found in plants, animals, and microorganisms are made of different combinations of twenty-two of these amino acids. Genes code the sequence of amino acids in a protein, and it is the sequence that dictates the protein's function. (*See* GENE.) Plants and some microorganisms are able to produce all the amino acids they need. Human beings and most other higher animals, however, cannot produce all the necessary amino acids. The eight amino acids that are not made by the body are called the essential amino acids. They must be supplied by food in the diet. (*See* DIET.) The essential amino acids are found in a variety of foods from animal and plant sources.

During digestion, certain types of enzymes called proteases break proteins into amino acids. These amino acids are small enough to be absorbed into the blood. They then travel to the tissues, where they are rebuilt into the new proteins that the body needs. Extra amino acids are not built into proteins, but are broken down again and converted into urea. Urea is then excreted as part of urine. *See also* DIGESTION; ENZYME; EXCRETION; UREA; URINE.

A.J.C./E.R.L.; L.O.S.; E.D.W.

AMMETER (am′ēt′ər) An ammeter is an instrument for measuring electric current. The measurement is usually in amperes. (*See* AMPERE.) There are three main kinds of ammeters.

The moving coil ammeter is like a galvanometer. (*See* GALVANOMETER.) It has a coil of wire between the poles of a permanent magnet. As electric current passes through the coil, it creates a magnetic field around the coil. The field of the coil and the field of the magnet make the coil move. A needle attached to the coil moves to show the amount the coil has moved. The distance it moves depends on how much current passes through the coil. The moving coil ammeter is designed for direct current, not alternating current. A rectifier is added to the moving coil ammeter if alternating current must be measured. (*See* RECTIFIER.)

The moving-iron ammeter has two pieces of iron inside a coil. One of the iron pieces can move. The other piece cannot move. The current passing through the coil produces a magnetic field. The force of the field moves one piece of iron away from the other. A needle on a scale shows how far apart the two pieces of iron move. The moving-iron ammeter can measure direct current or alternating current. It does not need a rectifier.

A hot-wire ammeter measures the heat produced by an electric current passing through it. The electric current heats a wire, causing it to expand. A needle is attached to indicate how much the wire expands.

Ammeters usually can be found wherever electrical power is in use. They are common in automobiles and appliances as well as larger machines that use electricity. *See also* ALTERNATING CURRENT; DIRECT CURRENT.

G.M.B./R.W.L.

AMMONIA (ə mō′nyə) Ammonia is a gas that is a compound of nitrogen and hydrogen. Its chemical formula is NH_3. It has a strong odor. Ammonia can be obtained by distilling coal into coke and coal gas. (*See* DISTILLATION.) Ammonia can also be made by combining hydrogen and nitrogen with a catalyst under pressure at a high temperature. This process is called the Haber-Bosch process. (*See* CATALYST.)

The ammonia used as a household cleaner is a strong solution of gas in water. Ammonia has many industrial uses. Because it can be broken down easily into hydrogen and nitrogen, ammonia is used to transport hydrogen. Ammonia was once widely used as a refrigerant but is now outdated. Smelling salts contain chemicals that release ammonia. The shock of the smell wakes up people who have fainted.

Ammonites were mollusks that lived millions of years ago. Some of them were huge, measuring more than 6 ft. (1.8 m) across. Many, like the one shown, were small.

Ammonia is also used to make ammonium compounds. It is used to make nitric acid and to dissolve certain substances. Salts of ammonia can be made by adding ammonia to an acid. These salts are called ammonium salts. The ammonia takes on a hydrogen atom to form an ammonium radical $(NH_4)+$. (*See* RADICAL; SALTS.) For example, ammonium chloride (NH_4Cl) is made by mixing ammonia (NH_3) and hydrochloric acid (HCl). The most important ammonium compound is ammonium sulfate. It is made from ammonia (NH_3) and sulfuric acid (H_2SO_4). It is used as a fertilizer because it provides nitrogen for the soil. Ammonium chloride, also called sal ammoniac, is used in the manufacture of dry cell batteries. It is also used in dyeing and printing. Ammonium nitrate is used in fertilizers, explosives, and in making nitrous oxide, sometimes called "laughing gas." *See also* NITROUS OXIDE.

J.J.A./A.D.

AMMONITE (am′ə nīt′) Ammonites were members of a large group of mollusks that lived millions of years ago. (*See* MOLLUSCA.)

They are now extinct. They resembled a modern mollusk, the nautilus. Most ammonites had coiled shells, so the group was named after the Egyptian god, Ammon, who had coiled horns. Ammonites are found as fossils in rocks ranging from Lower Jurassic to Upper Cretaceous in age. *See also* CEPHALOPOD; FOSSIL; GEOLOGICAL TIME SCALE.

S.R.G./W.R.S.

AMNIOCENTESIS (am′nē ō sen tē′səs) Amniocentesis is a test done on a pregnant woman by a medical doctor to find out if the fetus (unborn baby) is healthy and developing properly. Amniocentesis is not routinely done on all pregnant women. Doctors perform amniocentesis when the baby is at risk because of the mother's advanced age or because of the parents' genes.

Inside a pregnant woman's uterus, the fetus is surrounded by a thin layer of tissue called the amniotic sac. The sac contains fluid that includes cells shed by the fetus. During amniocentesis, a long, hollow needle is placed through the mother's abdomen into her uterus and the amniotic sac. A small amount of the amniotic fluid is taken out through the needle. The cells in the fluid are allowed to grow in a laboratory and are later examined. By performing the test, doctors can tell if the baby has any of more than one hundred disorders, such as Down's syndrome or hemophilia. The doctor can also tell if the fetus is a male or female.

Amniocentesis is generally safe for both the mother and the fetus and is most commonly performed late in the fourth month of pregnancy. Amniocentesis helps the doctor plan treatment if necessary after the baby is born. Doctors are even beginning to inject therapeutic drugs or perform corrective surgery on some fetuses before birth. If the fetus has a condition that cannot be treated and might cause it to die, some parents choose to end the pregnancy by an abortion. Other tests are being developed that would detect problems earlier than amniocentesis can. *See also* ABORTION; GENETICS; PREGNANCY.   P.W./J.E.P.

AMOEBA *See* AMEBA.

AMPERE (am′pir) The ampere, named after the French physicist André Ampère, is the basic unit used to measure the flow of an electric current. (*See* AMPÈRE, ANDRÉ.) Its symbol is A.

Electric current flows at the rate of 1 ampere when 1 coulomb flows past a section of an electric circuit in 1 second. The coulomb is an amount of electricity equal to the charge of 6.24×10^{18} electrons. In other words, 1 ampere equals 1 coulomb per second. (*See* COULOMB.)

The difference between a coulomb and an ampere lies in the difference between quantity and rate. For instance, a container may hold ten quarts of water. This is the container's quantity. A faucet may pour out a quart of water per minute. This is the rate. There is a coulomb, or quantity, of electricity. There is also an ampere, or rate, of electricity.

Electric current is measured with an ammeter. (*See* AMMETER.) A 100-watt light bulb requires about 1 ampere of current if the voltage is about 100 volts.

Physicists define amperes in terms of the magnetic force, measured in newtons, a current produces. In electrochemistry, the amperes the standard current depositing silver at the rate of 0.001118 grams per second when passed through a solution of silver nitrate.

Some scientific instruments use currents measured in microamperes, or millionths of amperes. Some large industrial equipment uses current measured in kiloamperes, or thousands of amperes. *See also* NEWTON; VOLT; WATT.   J.J.A./R.W.L.

AMPÈRE, ANDRÉ (1775-1836) André Ampère was a French physicist and mathematician. Ampère's greatest interest was in electricity. His work was the beginning of the new science of electrodynamics. Electrodynamics is the branch of physics having to do with the way electric currents affect each other.

Ampère discovered that two parallel electrical currents moving in the same direction attract each other. Two parallel currents going in opposite directions repel, or push each other away. He also discovered that current going through a coil wound up like a spring acts like a magnet. This kind of coil is called a solenoid. Ampère's experiments showed that electrical currents have the same effect as magnets. He invented the astatic needle. The astatic needle made it possible to discover and measure electric current.

Ampère suggested that the earth's magnetism might be caused by electrical currents going around in the earth's center. The ampere, the unit of electrical current, was named after him. *See also* AMPERE.   J.J.A./D.G.F.

AMPHETAMINE (am fet′ə mēn′) Amphetamines are human-made drugs. One example is the drug Benzedrine. Amphetamines are also called speed. They are stimulants. Doctors prescribe them for treatment of mild depression, alcoholism, and sleepiness. Because amphetamines increase metabolism, doctors sometimes prescribe them to help people lose weight. (*See* METABOLISM.) These are all legal and legitimate uses of the drugs.

Amphetamines are, however, common drugs of abuse. They are often obtained illegally and used by people who do not need them. Such use is dangerous because amphetamines can upset the functioning of the body. Amphetamines may cause restlessness, lack of sleep, irritability, and nausea. They can also cause damage to the nervous system and even death. People can become addicted to amphetamines. *See also* ADDICTION.   S.R.G./J.J.F.; M.H.M.

AMPHIBIAN (am fib′ē ən) An amphibian is a member of an ancient class of animals. The class came into existence about 350 million years ago. As a result of evolution, certain fish developed in such a way that they could breathe air and walk on land. The fins of some fish became legs. These fish evolved into amphibians. The name *amphibian* means "double life." Most early amphibians lived part of their life in water and the rest on land. After about 50 million years, some amphibians evolved into reptiles. Reptiles are a group of similar animals that can live away from water. (*See* REPTILE.) Although most amphibians disappeared, many have survived. Frogs, toads, and salamanders are amphibians.

Amphibians have backbones. Most of the adults have four legs. Even though all amphibians do not live in water, they do have to stay moist. The skin of humans prevents water from evaporating from their tissues. The skin of amphibians does not prevent evaporation. If the animal goes away from water on a hot day, it might dry up and die. Although most amphibians have lungs, they also breathe through their skin. Some salamanders breathe through gills, like fish. Amphibians lay eggs that must stay wet. Most amphibians lay eggs in water. Some of them, however, can lay their eggs in moist places such as under rotting logs and under leaves on the ground. The eggs that are laid in water hatch into tadpoles, or free-swimming larvae. (*See* LARVA.) Tadpoles live in the water and breathe through gills. When they change into adults, they can leave the water and breathe with lungs.

Amphibians are cold-blooded animals. This means that their body temperature does not remain at the same level at all times, but is the same temperature as their surroundings.

All amphibians alive today belong to one of three groups: apodans, urodeles, and anurans. The apodans are legless, wormlike creatures found only in tropical regions. Some species live in the water, but most burrow in damp soil.

The urodeles are amphibians with tails. Salamanders and newts are urodeles. Many urodeles are completely terrestrial; they do not have to return to water. There are other salamanders that never leave the water, such as the mud puppy and the axolotl of North America. Some salamanders live in dark caves and do not have eyes. The largest amphibian is the giant salamander of Japan, which is 5.5 ft. [1.65 m] long.

The anurans are the toads and frogs. They have hind legs that they use for jumping. Anurans vary in size from tiny tree frogs less than 1 in. [2.5 cm] long to the goliath frog of tropical Africa, which reaches a length of about 3.3 ft. [1 m] with its legs extended. Most anurans breed in the water and lay jellylike masses or strings of eggs. Frogs and toads eat insects, which they capture with their long, sticky tongues. Most frogs stay in or near water. Most toads, however, can travel away from water.   S.R.G./C.J.C.

AMPLIFIER (am′plə fī′ər) An amplifier is an electronic device that increases the strength

AMPHIBIANS

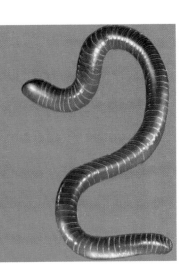

APODANS (CAECILIANS)

Among the most primitive of living amphibians, the apodans are mostly burrowing animals. They live in the tropics. They are legless and have very small eyes, both of these features being adaptations to underground life. Their ancestors had thick armored skin, and apodans still retain traces of this armor in the form of small plates embedded in their skin.

URODELES

The urodeles—the newts and salamanders—have kept the general shape of their ancestors, the first land animals. These pictures show that the newt tadpole and the frog tadpole are quite similar, even though the grown animals are very different. The resemblance of the larval stages is like the resemblance between embryos of certain mammals, such as rabbits and humans. The axolotl is really a giant tadpole, which can turn into a salamander. Some relatives of the axolotl, however, stay always as tadpoles, giving birth to young tadpoles. This is an example of neoteny.

ANURANS

The anurans—the frogs and toads—are amphibians specialized for jumping. Toads usually have warty skins, while frogs have smooth skins— otherwise there is little difference between them. Unlike other amphibians, anurans have voices, ranging from the high peeping of some tree frogs to the deep croak of the bullfrog. Anurans are protected from their enemies by slimy skin substances. The skin slime of the Kokoi frog of South America is one of the most deadly poisons known.

or power of a signal. Today, most amplifiers consist of integrated circuits and transistors. Vacuum tubes are used in some amplifiers when very high power is needed. (*See* INTEGRATED CIRCUIT; TRANSISTOR; VACUUM TUBE.)

Amplification occurs in stages. Each integrated circuit, tube, or transistor strengthens the signal that passes through it. Microphones, radio antennas, and the pickups in home stereo systems produce weak signals. These are usually fluctuating voltages. They may be as little as one millionth of a volt. (*See* VOLT.) Amplifiers must be used to boost the power of these signals so they can be heard. Amplifiers are particularly important in public-address systems. These systems are used when sound signals must reach many people in large rooms, or outdoors. Amplifiers used to produce high-quality sound in stereo systems are often expensive, complicated devices. *See also* ANTENNA; ELECTRONICS; RADIO.   P.Q.F.; W.R.P./L.L.R.

AMPLITUDE (am′plə tüd) Amplitude is the maximum distance a swinging or vibrating body moves from its place of rest, called its zero point. Amplitude is commonly used to measure the peak, or intensity, of sound waves and alternating electrical currents. Amplitude may also refer to the height of ocean waves. A good example of amplitude is the movement of a simple pendulum, such as a weight attached to the end of a piece of string. If the weight is pulled aside and released, it will swing to and fro, or oscillate. The greatest distance the weight travels in either direction from its original resting point is its amplitude. *See also* ALTERNATING CURRENT; SOUND; WAVE.   W.R.P./L.L.R.

ANACONDA (an′ə kän′də) The anaconda is one of the largest snakes in the world. The anaconda is a member of the Boidae family. It is found in the northern countries of South America. It may grow as long as 30 ft. [9 m] and as thick as an adult human's body. Unlike poisonous snakes, the anaconda does not kill its prey by biting. It wraps its body around its prey and suffocates the animal by squeezing it. Anacondas feed mostly on small mammals and birds. Sometimes they catch and swallow a caiman, which is a relative of the alligator. After the animal is dead, the anaconda swallows it whole. The anaconda spends much of its time in water. *See also* BOA.   S.R.G./C.J.C.

ANAEROBE (an′ə rōb′) An anaerobe is an organism that does not use oxygen in order to live and reproduce. Anaerobes do not carry

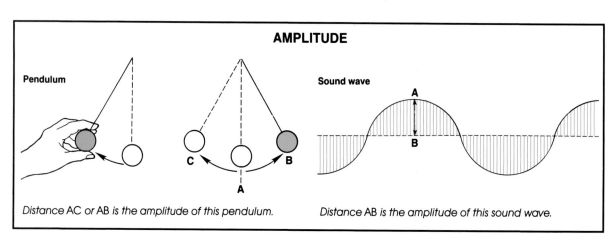
Distance AC or AB is the amplitude of this pendulum.   *Distance AB is the amplitude of this sound wave.*

out the process of respiration. (*See* RESPIRATION.) Many bacteria, fungi, and protozoans are anaerobic. They get their energy by breaking down either organic (carbon-containing) or inorganic compounds in a process called fermentation. (*See* FERMENTATION.) Some yeasts, for example, convert sugar into alcohol by fermentation.

Obligate anaerobes are organisms that must live in a totally oxygen-free environment. If exposed to oxygen, they will die. Facultative anaerobes can live either with or without oxygen. *See also* AEROBE.   A.J.C./E.R.L.

ANALGESIC (an′l jē′zik) An analgesic is a drug that reduces pain without causing unconsciousness or complete loss of feeling. Mild analgesics, such as acetaminophen, aspirin, and codeine, are used to relieve headaches, symptoms of arthritis, or other body pains. More powerful analgesics include substances derived from opium, called narcotics. Two such analgesics are morphine and heroin. These are dangerous drugs that can lead to addiction. They are used by doctors only for relieving intense pain of patients who are suffering from cancer or severe injuries. Many analgesics are also antipyretics, drugs that reduce fever. *See also* ANESTHETIC.

S.R.G./J.J.F.; M.H.M.

ANATOMY (ə nat′ə mē) is the study of how living things are built. The word *anatomy* comes from the Greek words that mean "cutting up." Most of what is known about how an organism is put together was learned by someone who cut it apart—that is, dissected it—and looked at it. Today, scientists can also study the inside of a living body with radiation and ultrasound. Anatomy is very important in the education of a doctor.

There are many different types of anatomy. In gross anatomy, the naked eye is used to study large parts of a body. In microscopic anatomy, microscopes are used to study very small parts of a body. Comparative anatomy is the study and comparison of similar parts of bodies in different species. A comparative anatomist may compare the heart of a fish, a frog, a snake, and a bird. Embryology is the study of embryos, which are developing unborn babies. Histology is the study of the structure of tissues. Cytology is the study of the structure of cells. (*See* CYTOLOGY; HISTOLOGY.)

The study of the structure of the human body is called human anatomy. By understanding the parts of the human body and how they are built, doctors are able to heal injuries and cure diseases. All the parts of a body work together in a very complicated way to keep a person alive. Although doctors and scientists now know much about the human body, they still do not understand how every part works.

The body is made up of nearly 50 million million cells. These cells are grouped together in different types of tissues, which have different functions. There are skin tissue, muscle tissue, bone tissue, and other kinds of tissue. Tissues are grouped together and form organs, such as the brain, heart, and stomach. Each cell works with other cells, and tissues and organs work within systems to do certain jobs such as digest food and deliver nutrients throughout the body. (*See* CELL; TISSUE; ORGAN.)

The skeletal system, or skeleton, is made up of all the bones in the body. There are 206 bones in the human body. They are connected in several ways. Two bones may move over each other at a special point called a joint. For example, the knee is the joint between the upper and lower leg bones. (*See* SKELETON.) The muscular system is made up of all the muscles. They are attached to the bones. The muscles move the bones and allow a person to move about in various ways. (*See* MUSCLE.)

The circulatory system is made up of the heart, arteries, veins, and blood. The blood carries nutrients and oxygen to every cell in the body. It also carries certain waste products, including carbon dioxide, away from the cells. The heart pumps the blood throughout the body. The blood leaves the heart through arteries and returns to the heart through veins. (*See* CIRCULATORY SYSTEM.) The lymphatic system acts in a similar way to remove other waste products from tissues. (*See* LYMPHATIC SYSTEM.)

The respiratory system provides oxygen from the air for the blood. This occurs in the lungs. When a person inhales, he or she is taking in air that contains oxygen for the blood to carry to the cells. When a person exhales, he or she is releasing air that contains carbon dioxide that the blood has carried from the cells. (*See* RESPIRATORY SYSTEM.)

The digestive system provides nutrients for the blood to take to the cells. Food is brought into the body through the mouth and throat. In the stomach and small intestine, food is chemically changed into a form that the body can use. The blood carries the resulting nutrients from the small intestine to the cells. The unusable parts of the food are removed through the large intestine and anus. (*See* DIGESTION.) The kidneys, part of the excretory system, filter wastes and excess salts from the blood and store them in the bladder. When the bladder is full, its contents are passed out of the body in the form of urine. The skin also gets rid of some wastes through sweating. (*See* EXCRETION.)

The reproductive system allows the body to produce offspring. The gonads, or sex organs, produce sex cells—eggs in the female and sperm in the male. The sex cells form a fertilized egg when they combine. The fertilized egg subsequently develops into an embryo. Each body has two gonads. A male gonad is called a testicle. A female gonad is called an ovary. The penis of the male transfers sperm into the vagina of the female. A sperm and an egg may combine in one of the female's fallopian tubes. (*See* REPRODUCTIVE SYSTEM.)

Two systems control all of the other systems to see that they work properly. The nervous system sends signals to and receives signals from parts of the body by means of impulses. These impulses are similar to electricity. The system includes the brain, spinal cord, and nerves. (*See* NERVOUS SYSTEM.) The endocrine system sends signals to parts of the body by means of chemicals in the blood. (*See* ENDOCRINE.) These chemicals are called hormones. The endocrine system includes organs such as the pituitary gland, adrenal glands, and thyroid gland. *See also* PHYSIOLOGY.

S.R.G./M.J.C.; J.J.F.; M.H.M.

ANCHOVY (an′chō′vē) An anchovy is a small, herringlike, saltwater fish belonging to the family Engraulidae. (*See* HERRING.) There are more than one hundred species. Anchovies grow from 4 to 10 in. [10 to 25 cm] in length. They have large eyes and mouths. Anchovies are found all over the world and are especially abundant off the coasts of Peru and Chile. The fish is used to make animal feed, fish bait, and fertilizer. Some species of the fish are filleted, salted, packed in oil, and sold as a food delicacy.

S.R.G./E.C.M.

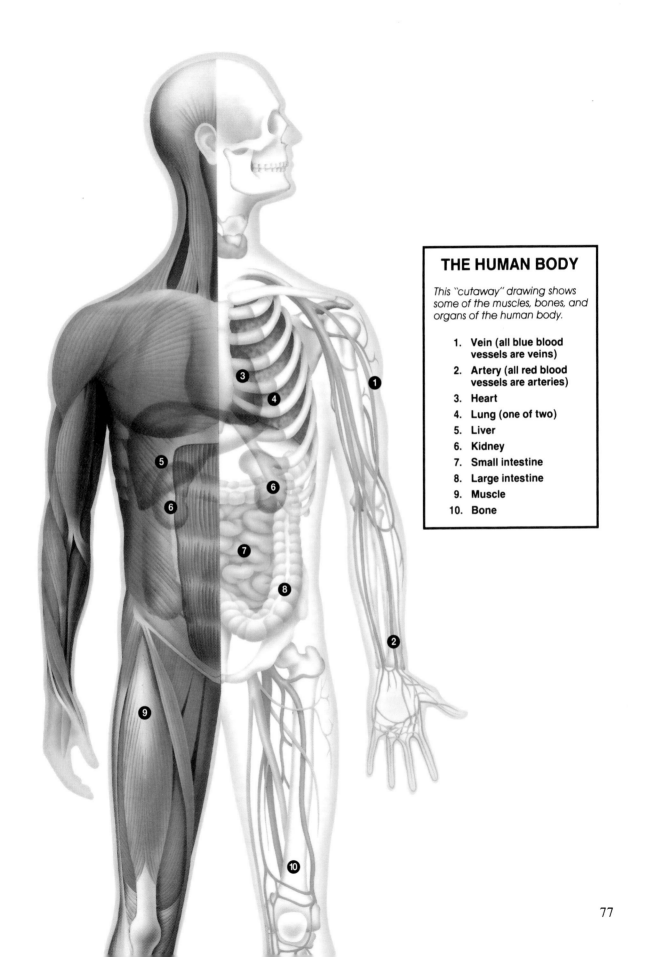

THE HUMAN BODY

This "cutaway" drawing shows some of the muscles, bones, and organs of the human body.

1. **Vein (all blue blood vessels are veins)**
2. **Artery (all red blood vessels are arteries)**
3. **Heart**
4. **Lung (one of two)**
5. **Liver**
6. **Kidney**
7. **Small intestine**
8. **Large intestine**
9. **Muscle**
10. **Bone**

ANDREWS, ROY CHAPMAN (1884-1960)
Roy Chapman Andrews was an American naturalist and explorer. He was born in Beloit, Wisconsin. He was an authority on whales. In 1906 he joined the staff of the Museum of Natural History in New York City, and he became its director in 1935. Andrews led six paleontological expeditions to Asia during the 1920s. (Paleontology is the study of fossils.) Among Andrews's most important discoveries were dinosaur eggs and the remains of large land mammals thought to have lived more than 90 million years ago. His writings include *On the Trail of Ancient Man* (1926) and *Quest of the Snow Leopard* (1955). P.Q.F./M.J.C.

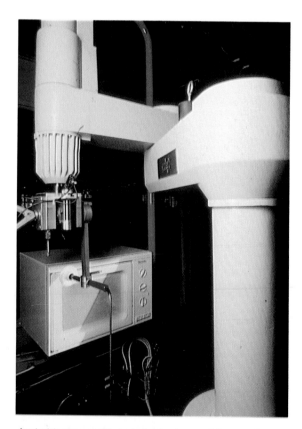

Androids are used in industry to do repetitive and/or hazardous tasks. The android above checks microwave ovens for microwave leaks.

ANDROID (an′drȯid′) An android, or automaton, is a machine that can be designed to imitate a limited range of human actions. Unlike a true robot, however, it cannot be reprogrammed to perform a variety of tasks. (*See* ROBOTICS.)

The first androids were made hundreds of years ago in Europe. They were art objects, most often clocks with humanlike figures that rang bells or made sounds.

The so-called androids in science-fiction stories are imaginary devices. Some have the characteristics of robots, whereas others, made entirely of biologic materials, are meant to be indistinguishable from human beings.

P.Q.F./E.W.L.

ANEMIA (ə nē′mē ə) Anemia is a condition in which there is a decrease in either the quantity of red blood cells or in the amount of hemoglobin in a person's blood. Red blood cells pick up oxygen in the lungs and carry the oxygen to body tissues. Hemoglobin is an iron-containing protein that is carried in the red blood cells. Hemoglobin gives blood its red color and makes it possible for the blood to carry oxygen. (*See* BLOOD; HEMOGLOBIN.)

Anemia has a number of different causes. Excessive blood loss—for example, from a wound— is one possible cause. In other cases, the bone marrow does not produce enough red blood cells because of a deficiency of a certain nutrient. If a person does not get enough iron, vitamin B_{12}, or folic acid in the diet—or if the body cannot absorb these nutrients properly—inadequate production of red blood cells may result. Pernicious anemia, for example, results from a deficiency of vitamin B_{12}. Aplastic anemias occur when the bone marrow loses its ability to produce red blood cells because of diseases such as leukemia (a form of cancer), exposure to certain chemicals, or exposure to radiation.

Normally, old red blood cells are destroyed in the liver, but more slowly than new red blood cells are produced. If destruction occurs too fast, anemia can result. Too-fast destruction may be caused by hereditary diseases, such as sickle-cell anemia, that produce abnormal red blood cells. Such cells are destroyed more quickly than normal red blood cells. (*See* SICKLE-CELL ANEMIA.)

Some common symptoms of anemia are feeling tired all the time, being short of breath, and having abnormally pale skin. To cure anemia, doctors treat its cause. For example, a person may need to take iron or vitamin supplements.   S.R.G./J.J.F.; M.H.M.; L.O.S.

ANEMOMETER (an′ə mäm′ət ər) An anemometer is an instrument that tells how fast the wind is blowing. The simplest anemometer, known as the Robinson's anemometer, has three or four cups attached to a vertical pipe. The wind catches the cups, spinning them around. The wind's speed is measured by how many times the cups go around in a certain period of time. Two other kinds, the hot wire anemometer and the pressure plate anemometer, give more exact recordings of wind speeds.

The cup anemometer is used to measure wind speed. When the wind blows against the cups, the cups rotate on their shaft. As the speed of the wind changes, so does the speed of rotation of the cups. A gauge on the shaft measures the number of rotations.

Airplane pilots and sailors need to know the speed of the wind. A meteorologist needs to use an anemometer when making a weather forecast. *See also* WEATHER.   J.J.A./C.R.

ANESTHETIC (an′əs thet′ik) An anesthetic is a substance that causes loss of feeling in the body. A local anesthetic causes the loss of feeling in a small part of the body, such as a finger. Local anesthetics work by blocking the nerves that carry pain messages from various parts of the body to the brain. A general anesthetic causes loss of feeling throughout the entire body. General anesthetics work in the brain itself to shut off perception of all sensations. Unconsciousness usually occurs when a general anesthetic is used.

Anesthetics are used by doctors to stop pain. When a cut has to be stitched closed, a doctor will inject a local anesthetic so that the patient will not feel the pain of the stitching. The patient remains awake and alert. When more extensive surgery is necessary, such as an operation to remove an appendix, a doctor will give the patient a general anesthetic. This will stop all pain and keep the patient asleep until the operation is over. A physician called an anesthesiologist is trained to give the proper amount of anesthetic to patients.

Common general anesthetics are nitrous oxide ("laughing gas"), halothane, and sodium pentothal ("truth serum"). Common local anesthetics are lidocaine and procaine. The use of anesthetics was first suggested by Sir Humphry Davy in 1799. They were first used, in 1844, by the American dentist Horace Wells. *See also* DAVY, SIR HUMPHRY; NITROUS OXIDE; PROCAINE.

S.R.G./J.J.F.; M.H.M.

ANEURYSM (an′yə′riz əm) An aneurysm is an enlargement of a blood vessel. Aneurysms can cause severe pain, especially if they rupture, or break. When an aneurysm ruptures, it produces a hemorrage, or uncontrollable bleeding. If a hemorrhage occurs in the heart or aorta, the main artery leading from the heart, death can occur. Aneurysms can put pressure on organs even if they do not rupture. This is particularly serious when pressure is put on a part of the brain.

Aneurysms can have many causes. These include birth defects, certain infections, high blood pressure, and injuries. Aneurysms can be detected by X rays and treated by surgery. A small vessel with an aneurysm can be removed or tied off to prevent the flow of blood through it. A large vessel can be replaced by another vessel. The large vessel is removed, and a vessel from another part of the body is surgically implanted. A large vessel also may be repaired through grafting. In grafting, the aneurysm is cut out of the vessel, and body tissue from another part of the body is placed over the hole. *See also* HEART.

P.Q.F./J.E.P.

ANGELFISH Angelfish is the name of several colorful fishes, some of which live in fresh water and some of which live in salt water. One kind of angelfish is also called the scalare. It has a very narrow, deep body with large fins. It is a very pretty fish and is often kept in aquariums. S.R.G./E.C.M.

ANGIOGRAPHY (an′jē äg′rə fe) Angiography is an X-ray procedure that examines the body's blood vessels. Angiography helps a doctor determine whether a blood vessel is blocked or diseased.

When angiography is performed, a thin, flexible tube called a catheter is inserted into a particular place on the patient's body. A substance called a contrast medium is injected through the catheter. X rays are then directed at the part of the body being studied. (*See* X RAY.) The X-ray machine is connected to a

television monitor. The radiologist (physician trained in the use of radiation) watches the monitor. (*See* RADIOLOGY.) The contrast medium highlights the blood vessels in the image, making them easier to see. Sometimes, the images are videotaped for the radiologist to examine again later. The X-ray images that result from the angiographs are called angiograms. There are several different types of angiograms. For example, a cerebral angiogram is an image of the blood vessels in the head. A coronary angiogram is an image of the blood vessels in the heart.

A newer type of angiography is called digital subtraction angiography. Digital subtraction angiography (DSA) uses a computer. Two images are made of the same organ. The first image is made before the contrast medium is injected. The second is made after the contrast medium is injected. The computer subtracts the first image from the second to make a third image. This third image shows a clear picture of only the blood vessels.

P.W./J.E.P.

ANGIOPLASTY (an′jē ə plast′ē) Angioplasty is a procedure used to clear arteries of the heart that are blocked by deposits called plaques. (*See* ARTERIOSCLEROSIS.) A catheter, or very narrow tube, with a tiny, collapsed balloon at the tip is inserted into an artery in the arm or the upper part of the inner thigh. The catheter is moved toward the heart and finally to the artery that is blocked. There, the balloon is inflated by a pump that is attached to the other end of the catheter. The balloon expands, compressing the blockage and clearing a wider opening through which the blood can flow. The balloon is then deflated, and the balloon and catheter are taken out of the body.

Angioplasty was introduced in 1977 by Dr. Andreas Gruntzig of the University of Zurich in Switzerland. Before then, doctors had used only open-heart bypass surgery to repair blocked arteries. In bypass surgery, a vein, usually taken from the patient's leg, is surgically implanted near the heart to route blood around the blockage. Angioplasty can be an alternative to bypass surgery for patients with certain conditions. *See also* HEART; HEART DISEASE.   P.W./J.E.P.

ANGIOSPERM (an′jē ə spərm′) An angiosperm is any plant that grows flowers. *Angiosperm* is another name for all the plants of the division Anthophyta. Not all angiosperms produce flowers that are bright and colorful like those found in gardens. For example, even the grass in a lawn grows flowers. Grass flowers are small and green, so they are rarely noticed. Grass, like other angiosperms, also bears fruit, which develops from the flowers. All of an angiosperm's seeds are found inside its fruit.

Angiosperms are the most common type of plant on earth. There are more than 250,000 species. There are two groups of angiosperms: monocotyledons and dicotyledons. Monocotyledons have long, narrow leaves, flower parts in groups of three, and seeds with one leaf inside. Dicotyledons have wide leaves, flower parts in groups of four or five, and seeds with two leaves inside. *See also* DICOTYLEDON; FLOWER: MONOCOTYLEDON; PLANT KINGDOM.   S.R.G./M.J.C.; M.H.S.

ANGSTROM UNIT An angstrom (ang′strəm) unit is an extremely small unit of length. It is equal to one ten billionth of a meter. Its symbol is A. Angstrom units are used to measure very

Common angiosperms, or flowering plants, include oak trees (below left) which produce nuts called acorns. Roses produce beautiful, fragrant flowers (below middle). Tomato plants produce prized fruits (below right). Grasses (bottom) include such crops as wheat, rye, and oats that produce tiny flowers.

short distances or lengths, such as the size of an atom. Scientists once used the angstrom to measure wavelengths of light rays, but they now use the nanometer. The nanometer is a unit of linear measure that is one billionth of a meter. The angstrom unit was named for Anders Angstrom, a Swedish physicist.

W.R.P./R.W.L.

ANHYDRIDE (an hī′drīd′) Anhydrides are chemical compounds from which water has been removed. For example, taking water (H_2O) out of sulfuric acid (H_2SO_4) makes an anhydride. It is called sulfur trioxide (SO_3.)

There are two kinds of anhydrides. An acid anhydride is what remains after water is taken out of an acid. A basic anhydride combines with water to form bases. (*See* ACID; BASE.)

Anhydrides are important in chemistry. They are used in making other compounds. One of the most important anhydrides is acetic anhydride. It can be made into acetic acid. *See also* ACETIC ACID.

J.J.A./A.D.

ANILINE (an′l ən) Aniline is a colorless, oily, poisonous liquid. It is made by reducing nitrobenzene. (*See* OXIDATION AND REDUCTION.) Aniline is used in the manufacture of rubber and drugs and in the making of dyes. The boiling point of aniline is 363.43°F. [184.13°C]. Its freezing point is 20.7°F. [-6.3°C]. Aniline has the formula $C_6H_5NH_2$.

J.J.A./J.M.

PROJECT

ANIMAL KINGDOM All animals are said to belong to the animal kingdom. Most animals can move. Most have eyes, legs, and a head. However, some simple animals do not have eyes, or legs, or a head. Some animals that live in the ocean look like plants. The sea anemone is an example of a plantlike animal. The easiest way to tell the difference between plants and animals is to see how they get their food. Plants make their own food by photosynthesis. (*See* PHOTOSYNTHESIS.) Animals cannot use photosynthesis. They must get their food by eating plants or other animals. A tiny worm and a huge whale have one thing in common. They cannot make their own food. They must find it and eat it.

There are over one million species of animals. Some live at the bottom of oceans. Some live at the top of mountains. Animals are found at the north pole and at the equator. Some species only have one cell. Others have billions of cells. A sponge is a very simple animal that sits in one place. A human being is a very complex animal that can move around. Biologists try to divide the members of the animal kingdom into smaller groups. They study the characteristics of each animal. Then they decide to which group it belongs.

Each animal in the animal kingdom belongs to a smaller group called a phylum. (*See* CLASSIFICATION OF LIVING ORGANISMS.) The following are major phyla in the animal kingdom: Porifera (sponges), Cnidaria (jellyfishes), Platyhelminthes (flatworms), Aschelminthes (roundworms), Mollusca (clams and octopuses), Annelida (segmented worms), Arthropoda (insects, crabs, shrimp, spiders), Echinodermata (starfish), and Chordata (all higher animals with nerve cords). Most of the familiar animals have nerve cords and backbones. They are also called vertebrates. Fish, frogs, birds, dogs, cats, and humans are all examples of vertebrates, members of Chordata. Animals that do not have backbones are called invertebrates.

The study of animals and the animal kingdom is called zoology. A scientist who studies zoology is called a zoologist. *See also* INVERTEBRATE; KINGDOM; VERTEBRATE; ZOOLOGY. S.R.G./R.J.B.; M.J.C.

ANION (an′ī′ən) An anion is a negatively charged ion. Anions were discovered and named in 1834 by Michael Faraday, a British chemist. (*See* FARADAY, MICHAEL.)

Anions carry a specific number of negative electric charges. For example, the chlorine ion (Cl^-) has an electric charge of one, meaning it is a univalent anion. The sulfate ion ($SO_4^=$) has a negative electric charge of 2. It is a bivalent anion.

Anions move toward the positive electrode, or anode, during electrolysis. *See also* ELECTROLYSIS; IONS AND IONIZATION; VALENCE. J.J.A./A.D.

ANNEALING (ə nēl′ing) Annealing is the manufacturing process by which molten metal or glass are gradually cooled. Controlled cooling of steel, for example, softens it and makes it more ductile, or easier to work with. Cooling is done first in a furnace, then in air. Glass is cooled slowly in annealing ovens to prevent stains and bubbles caused by carbon dioxide. Slow cooling allows heat to drive off the carbon dioxide.

Quenching and tempering are two other steel-making processes related to annealing. In quenching, the steel is heated to a critical temperature. (*See* CRITICAL TEMPERATURE.) It is then plunged into water or oil for quick cooling. This makes the steel strong, hard, and brittle. In tempering, steel is reheated to a temperature just below the critical temperature, and then cooled slowly. This softens the steel and increases its toughness. *See also* STEEL; HEAT TREATMENT. W.R.P./A.D.

ANNELIDA (an′l əd ə) Annelida is a phylum containing a large group of invertebrate animals. There are three classes of annelids: Poly-

Of the four typical annelids shown, the earthworm (top) is perhaps the best known. The peacock worm and the ragworm are marine forms—that is, they live in the sea.

ANNELIDS

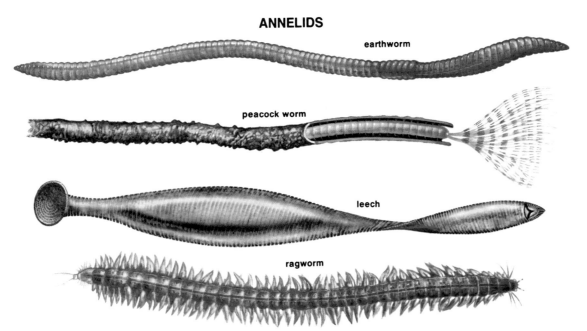

earthworm

peacock worm

leech

ragworm

chaeta (marine worms), Oligochaeta (earthworms), and Hirudinea (leeches). Annelids, or segmented worms, are much more complex than Platyhelminthes (flatworms) and Aschelminthes (roundworms). Their patterns of development resemble those of arthropods and mollusks. *See also* ANIMAL KINGDOM; INVERTEBRATE. S.R.G./C.S.H.

ANNUAL PLANT An annual (an'yü əl) plant is a plant that lives for only one growing season. It grows from a seed in the spring. It flowers in the summer. It scatters seeds and dies in the fall. The plants that appear the next spring grow from the seeds of the dead plant. Examples of annual plants are the bean, nasturtium, pea, petunia, radish, sunflower, sweet pea, and tomato. S.R.G./T.L.G.; M.H.S.

ANNUAL RING A circular line in the wood of a tree that shows how it has grown is called an annual (an'yü əl) ring. As a tree gets older, it grows taller and thicker. To grow thicker, a tree adds wood underneath its bark. In tropical regions where there is no winter, trees grow year-round. In places where there is a

The cross section of a tree trunk reveals important information to scientists. Each ring of a tree represents a year's growth.

cold winter, trees stop growing during the winter.

When growth stops in the fall, the wood cells are smaller than they are in the spring, when growth continues. If a tree is cut down and sawn straight across, the change from fall to spring growth appears as a circular line in the wood. There is one ring in the wood for each year the tree has grown. The age of a tree can be told by counting the rings on its stump after the tree has been cut down.

Scientists learn about weather conditions in the past by studying the width of annual rings. The annual ring produced in a dry year is narrow. The annual ring produced in a wet year is wide. *See also* DATING. S.R.G./M.H.S.

ANODIZING (an'ə dīz'ing) Anodizing is a way of coating certain metals with an oxide film. This film resists corrosion. Aluminum and magnesium are the metals most often anodized. Sometimes, zinc is anodized. (*See* CORROSION; OXIDE.)

The natural oxide film on aluminum is thin. Anodizing makes a thicker oxide layer. This protects the aluminum from corrosion and makes it last longer.

In anodizing, aluminum is used as the positively charged electrode of an electrolytic cell. Electrolytes such as sulfuric acid are used. (*See* ELECTROLYSIS.) The oxide layer forms from the metal surface outward. This results in the outside layer being slightly rough and porous. It must be sealed by boiling it in water. This prevents harmful substances from attacking the metal.

Anodizing with sulfuric acid makes a clear oxide film. With chromic acid, a dull film is produced. The film may be dyed for decorative purposes. Chromic acid is also used for anodizing zinc. J.J.A./A.D.

ANOREXIA NERVOSA (an′ə rek′sē ə nər-vō′sə) Anorexia nervosa is an eating disorder in which a person refuses to eat. Anorexia nervosa occurs mostly in females who are adolescents or young adults. The anorexic may seem to act normally and may even be a "model" student. Symptoms of anorexia nervosa include loss of 25 percent of body weight, excessive fear of being fat, distorted body image, and a preoccupation with food and exercise. Because the anorexic's body is so underweight, she may also have low blood pressure, body temperature, and heart rate; extreme sensitivity to cold; and weakened muscles.

The anorexic is driven to lose weight because of personal stress and beliefs by society that thinness is beautiful. The anorexic starves herself and compulsively exercises to become thin, even though her weight may be normal. Anorexics also may suffer from bulimia. Bulimia is an eating disorder that involves overeating in secret, followed by self-induced vomiting. (*See* BULIMIA.)

Treatment for anorexia nervosa can involve hospitalization or psychological therapy. An anorexic may remain in the hospital for weeks or even years. While in the hospital, the patient may be fed through tubes. Therapists work with anorexics to solve problems such as depression, feelings of helplessness, low self-esteem, and guilt. Many recovered anorexics are still uncomfortable with eating and their body image. The disorder has a high relapse rate and a high death rate.   P.W./J.E.P.

ANT Ants are insects that belong to the order Hymenoptera. There are many thousands of species of ants. They are different sizes. Most ants, however, are smaller than 1 in. [2.5 cm] long. Ants are found in most parts of the world. They are related to bees.

Ants are social animals. This means that they live together in large colonies, or groups. Some colonies may contain millions of ants. Most colonies make nests in the ground or in dead trees. Others do not make nests. The army ants of the tropical jungles march to a

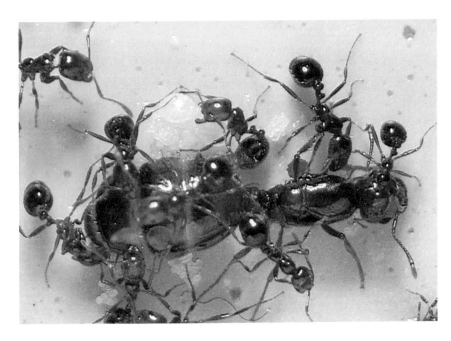

There are thousands of different kinds of ants. A queen fire ant and some of the workers attending her are pictured. Fire ants are serious pests in southern areas of the United States.

different place every day. Thousands of them march in a narrow band and eat any animal that cannot get out of their way. Army ants can eat all the flesh of an animal very quickly.

There are different types of ants in each colony. Usually there is only one queen ant, a female that is the most important insect in the colony. The queen is the only ant that can lay eggs. When the eggs are fertilized by males, the eggs hatch into female worker ants. When the eggs are not fertilized by males, they hatch into more male ants. (*See* PARTHENOGENESIS.) Although there are thousands of worker ants in each colony, there are few male ants in a colony. Queen and male ants have wings. The queen and a male ant mate while flying in the air. Worker ants do not have wings. Worker ants collect food, feed the young ants, and build the nest. Some species of ants also have female soldier ants. They protect the nest.

Ants can do many things. They are able to travel long distances away from their nest and find their way back, because they follow their own chemical trails. Some ants can also grow food. They chew up leaves and store them in their nests. When a fungus grows on the leaves, they harvest the fungus for food. They also eat a sugary substance produced by aphids. Some species of ants keep aphids in almost the same way that humans keep milk cows. (*See* APHID.) Ants are very strong. They can lift things much larger than themselves. They can lift things that weigh fifty times as much as they do. To match this, a person weighing 200 lb. [91 kg] would have to lift 10,000 lb. [4,536 kg].   S.R.G./J.R.

ANTARES See STAR.

ANTEATER (ant′ēt ər) The anteater is a furry mammal. (*See* MAMMAL.) It belongs to

the order Edentata, which means "toothless." The anteater has a long, sticky tongue. Its snout is long and slender. With its powerful claws, it rips open the nests of insects. It eats ants and termites. Most anteaters are nocturnal animals. They come out mostly at night. The giant anteater is diurnal. It comes out mostly in the day. Anteaters live alone.

Some anteaters, like this collared anteater, climb trees. Anteaters use their long, sticky tongue to capture ants and termites.

There are three kinds of anteaters: the giant anteater, the collared anteater, and the silky (or two-toed) anteater. The giant anteater is about 7 ft. [2.1 m] long from the end of its tail to the tip of its nose. It wanders the forest floor in search of food. The collared anteater is about 3.3 ft. [1 m] long. It gets its name from the coloration of fur around its shoulders, chest, and neck. The collared anteater climbs in trees and can hold onto branches with its tail. The silky anteater is 18 in. [45.7 cm] long. It also climbs trees and uses its tail for holding. The silky anteater is sometimes called the two-toed anteater. G.M.B./J.J.M.

ANTELOPE (ant′l ōp′) The antelope is a four-legged, hairy mammal that belongs to the family Bovidae. Antelopes are a type of ungulate, which is an animal with hooves. (*See* MAMMAL; UNGULATE.) Antelopes are found in Africa and Asia, usually in large herds. They are all ruminants. (*See* RUMI-NANT.) This means they are cud-chewers. They swallow their food without having completely chewed it. Later this food is brought back up and rechewed as cud. Then it is swallowed again. Like most ruminants, antelopes have four-part stomachs.

Most antelopes are swift, delicate animals. They range in size, at shoulder height, from about 1 ft. [0.3 m] to about 6 ft. [2 m]. The smallest antelope is the royal antelope (*Neotragus pygmaeus*). The largest is the eland. (*See* ELAND.)

Both the male and female antelope may have horns. The horns on the female are usually smaller than those of the male.

Two of the best-known species of antelopes are the gnu and the impala. (*See* GNU; IMPALA.) Antelopes provide a major food source for the large African and Asiatic carnivores (meat eaters). People also use the flesh of the antelope for food. The hide is often used for clothing, blankets, rugs, or ornamental purposes.   J.J.A./J.J.M.

Antelopes live in large herds in the grasslands of Africa and Asia. Although they are fast runners, antelopes are often preyed upon by lions and tigers.

ANTENNA (an ten′ə) An antenna is a piece of equipment for sending and receiving electromagnetic radiation. It is a basic part of all electronic communication systems. It is used for radio, television, radar, and radio telescope operations. An antenna is also called an aerial. (*See* RADAR; RADIO; RADIO ASTRONOMY; TELEVISION.)

These antennas allow the ship on which they are mounted to communicate with any part of the world. Antennas are a basic part of all electronic communication systems.

There are two basic kinds of antennas. A dipole antenna has two pieces of metal or wire. A monopole antenna has a single metal or wire conductor that may be attached at one end. Antennas come in many shapes and sizes. Radio transmission antennas may be tall towers. Receiving antennas for transistor radios may be no bigger than a fingernail. Locations of antennas also vary. For example, some antennas, such as those for television transmitters, must be put on the tallest buildings or the highest land peaks.

The kind of antenna used depends on the type of electronic signal it sends or receives. Some signals require loop, or round, antennas. Other signals require vertical or horizontal

Arthropods, such as this shrimp, sense their environment with their antennae. Tiny hairs growing from arthropods' antennae are sensitive to such things as taste, feel, movement, and smell.

antennas. The design of an antenna must match the frequency or wavelength of its signal. AM radio antennas are used for low-frequency signals. Low-frequency signals have long wavelengths. Television antennas are used for high-frequency signals. High-frequency signals have short wavelengths. Radar and radio telescope antennas are used for very high-frequency signals. Very high-frequency signals have very short wavelengths called microwaves. (*See* MICROWAVE.)

The first antenna was built by Heinrich Hertz, a German physicist, about 1887. His work with an antenna led to the invention of radio transmission and reception by Guglielmo Marconi, an Italian engineer, in 1896. *See also* MARCONI, GUGLIELMO; ELECTRICITY; HERTZ, HEINRICH.　　　　G.M.B./L.L.R.

ANTENNAE (an ten'ē') Antennae are sense organs of insects and other arthropods. (*See* ARTHROPODA.) The antennae project from the animals' heads and are used mainly for touching, smelling, or hearing. Tiny hairlike nerves in the antennae pick up sensations.

Ants use their antennae to follow a scent. The silk moth can use its antennae to smell another silk moth that may be many miles away. Insects that live in darkness often use their antennae to avoid bumping into things. Some small crustaceans use their antennae to move themselves through water.　　G.M.B./J.R.

ANTHER (an'thər) An anther is part of the stamen (male part) of a flower. (*See* STAMEN.) The anther contains the pollen, which is used in reproduction. The anther is connected to the flower by a slender stalk, called a filament. Anthers usually have four swollen parts containing pollen. When the pollen is ripe, the swollen parts of the anther break open. This releases the pollen. Some anthers open with a small explosion. The explosion blows the pollen into the air. Otherwise, the pollen stays on the anther. In either case, the wind may then blow the pollen away. Sometimes pollen from the anther sticks on the hairs of insects. They carry it away to other flowers. *See also* POLLINATION.   J.J.A./M.H.S.

Anthers, shown here in a lily, are the pollen-producing parts of flowering plants. They are located at the ends of the stamens, or male parts, of flowers.

ANTHERIDIUM (an'thə rid'ē əm) An antheridium is the male sex organ found on ferns, mosses, hornworts, liverworts, and some species of algae and fungi. Antheridia (plural of *antheridium*) are found on the upper surfaces of mosses, hornworts, and liverworts but are on the undersides of fern leaves. *See also* ARCHEGONIUM.   J.J.A/M.J.C.; M.H.S.

ANTHROPOID (an'thrə pȯid') An anthropoid is a highly developed mammal that is also a primate. (*See* PRIMATE.) Anthropoids form one of the two major groups of primates. Humans, the apes, and the monkeys belong to this group. Other primates are included in the prosimian group.

An anthropoid has a flattened face with eyes in the front of the skull. Its brain is relatively large in proportion to its body. An anthropoid has stereoscopic vision, which allows it to judge depths of distance.

G.M.B./M.H.S.

ANTHROPOLOGY (an'thrə pol'ə jē) Anthropology is the study of humankind. It deals with the way humans lived in the past and the way humans live today. It began as a science in the 1800s. Anthropology is an outgrowth of biology and the social sciences. It has three main divisions: physical anthropology, cultural anthropology, and prehistory.

Physical anthropology deals with the origin and development of the human species from a biological standpoint. It studies the skeletons of humans to learn how humans evolved and how we have changed. It also studies the differences between human beings who live in different places. The colors of hair and skin, the shapes of heads and bodies, and the different types of human blood are some of the things physical anthropologists study and compare.

Cultural anthropology deals with how and why humans behave as we do. Cultural anthropologists note such things as family and large-group structure. They study a society's customs, work habits, recreational pursuits, language, visual arts, crafts, music, and literature. They study the medicine, religion, and technology of particular societies.

Louis Leakey, a Kenyan of British descent, and Margaret Mead of the United States are two famous anthropologists. (*See* LEAKEY FAMILY; MEAD, MARGARET.) Leakey, a physical anthropologist, devoted most of his life to searching for the fossil remains of prehistoric humans. He discovered, in Africa, the skulls of humanlike creatures who lived millions of years ago. Margaret Mead, a cultural anthropologist, studied people who lived without a written language or machines. She spent many years in the islands of the South Pacific. *See also* ARCHEOLOGY; EVOLUTION; FOSSIL; HUMAN BEING.   G.M.B./S.O.

ANTIBIOTIC (ant′i bī ät′ik) Antibiotics are chemical substances that microooorganisms produce to protect themselves against harm from other living organisms. People often use antibiotics to control disease. The first antibiotic discovered was penicillin. In 1928, Alexander Fleming, a British scientist, found that a chemical secreted by a mold called *Penicillium notalum* had stopped the growth of bacteria in a laboratory culture. He named the antibiotic after the mold. (*See* BACTERIA; FLEMING, SIR ALEXANDER; PENICILLIN.)

Antibiotics work by several different means. Some antibiotics, such as penicillin, interfere with the ability of bacteria to make cell walls. This prevents these bacteria from growing and reproducing. Other antibiotics interfere with bacteria's ability to make proteins. If a bacteria cannot make proteins, it dies. Antibiotics that prevent bacteria from multiplying are called bacteriostatic, while those that kill bacteria are called bacteriocidal. Sometimes, through genetic means, bacteria can produce bacteria that are not affected by an antibiotic. These new bacteria are said to be resistant to the antibiotic.

In 1957, the chemical structure of penicillin was discovered. By making changes in that structure, scientists were able to make new varieties of the antibiotic. Bacteria that had become resistant to the original drug could be controlled successfully with one of the new penicillin strains.

In the 1940s, Selman Waksman, a Russian-American biologist, tested various organisms to find those that would produce antibiotics. As a result of his research, actinomycin, streptomycin, the tetracyclines, and other antibiotics were found. (*See* WAKSMAN, SELMAN ABRAHAM.) Penicillin, streptomycin, and the tetracyclines are called broad-spectrum antibiotics because they are effective in the treatment of many different kinds of infections. Some antibiotics are used only against particular diseases or microorganisms. These are called narrow-spectrum antibiotics. Actinomycin, for example, is used to prevent the growth of some cancers.

Antibiotics make up the most powerful group of drugs we have for controlling infectious disease. They are used most successfully against diseases caused by bacteria and rickettsiae, many of which were once extremely dangerous to people. (*See* RICKETTSIA.) It is because of the use of antibiotics that serious infectious diseases such as tuberculosis, dysentery, syphilis, and typhus can be controlled.

Sometimes antibiotics are used to prevent infection. They are usually given to a patient before he or she has surgery in which a foreign object, such as a metal kneecap, is to be left in the body.

Some antibiotics are fed to healthy poultry and livestock to make them grow faster and to keep them healthy. Using antibiotics in the food of healthy animals means that many bacteria are allowed to build up a resistance to

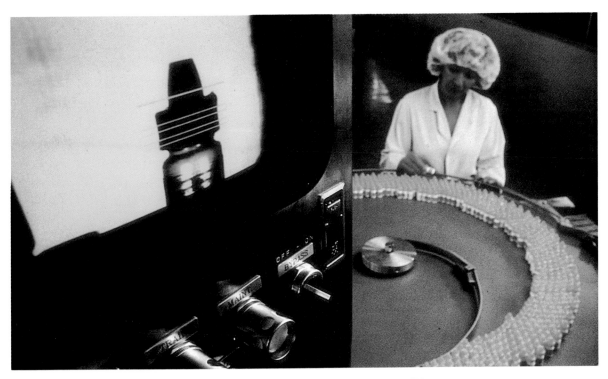

Like all drugs, antibiotics must be manufactured to exact standards. The monitor in this picture helps quality-control technicians assure that packaging equipment is working properly.

them. This means that the antibiotics will be less effective against disease. Almost half the antibiotics produced in the United States are used in this way. In some other countries, giving antibiotics to healthy animals is no longer legal.

Thousands of antibiotics have been developed, and nearly one hundred of those are used by doctors to treat various diseases in humans. Some are designed by chemists and then made synthetically (artificially).

Among the most recently developed antibiotics are amphoteicine b, nystatin, ampicillin, and the cephalesporins. The first two are used to treat fungus infections. Ampicillin is used against intestinal infections, among others. The cephalesporins are a group of synthetically made antibiotics and are an alternative for people who are allergic to penicillin. *See also* MICROORGANISM.   W.R.P./J.J.F.; M.H.M.

ANTIBODY (ant′i bäd′ē) An antibody is a protein made by a body's immune system. Antibody production is caused by the presence of antigens. Antigens are also proteins, but they do not belong in the body. These foreign substances are found in bacteria, viruses, insects, snake venom, and transplanted organs from another person. (*See* TRANSPLANTATION.) Both the antigens and the antibodies circulate in the blood.

Each antibody is made by the immune system to fight a particular kind of antigen. The antibodies that destroy one antigen will not usually affect another one. Antigens are destroyed because the antibodies bind closely with them. This binding of antigen to antibody is a signal for immune system cells to attack the antigen.

Once a certain kind of antigen has been destroyed, the body may have the ability to quickly produce more antibodies to fight a second attack, if needed. If this happens, the body has become immune to that antigen. (*See* IMMUNITY.) The person probably will not get the disease caused by the antigen again. This is the principle behind vaccination, in which antigens that are too weak to produce actual disease are injected into the body. The body starts producing antibodies, which quickly destroy the antigens. The body then has the ability to quickly make more of these antibodies, and so the person does not get the disease if exposed to it at a later time. Vaccinations have controlled the spread of many diseases, such as polio and measles. (*See* DISEASE; PATHOGEN; VACCINATION.)

Some antigens are poisons called toxins. Antibodies that neutralize these toxins are called antitoxins. (*See* ANTITOXIN.) For example, poisonous snakes have a strong toxin that they release through their fangs when they bite. The body of the bitten person starts to produce antitoxins to fight this poison. In some cases, the poison may be so strong that the body cannot produce enough antitoxins fast enough. Artificial antitoxins must be injected, or the person may die. A.J.C./J.J.F.; M.H.M.

ANTICLINE (ant′i klīn′) An anticline is a bending in layers of rock that make up the earth's crust. It is also called an upfold, which is a formation that looks like an upside down U. An anticline is caused by sideways (horizontal) forces from opposite directions. These forces, or pressures, push the rock upward. (*See* FOLDING; STRATIFICATION.)

Some anticlines contain rock that is folded up and down. An anticline with upfolds and downfolds is called an anticlinorium. An anticlinorium has one major upfold. It also has minor upfolds and downfolds.

Pictured above is a typical anticline, or as it is sometimes called, an upfold. Anticlines are caused by forces coming from opposite directions. These forces push the rock layers upward.

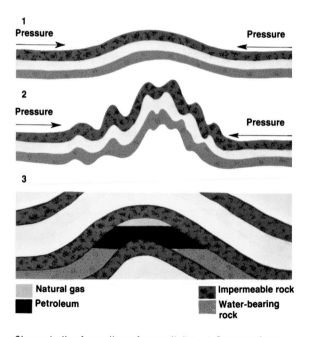

Stages in the formation of an anticline: 1. Pressure forms a simple anticline; 2. a complex anticline, or anticlinorium, forms; 3. the crest of an anticline may be eroded away, with the anticline sometimes continuing underground. Petroleum and natural gas may be trapped at the crest of a water-bearing rock layer that is enclosed by two impermeable (solid) rock layers.

An anticline is most often identified by the crest, or the top of the fold. Geologists also identify anticlines by comparing rock on opposite sides of the crest. If the rock on both sides is the same, usually the structure is an anticline.

Geologists used to think that anticlines were the most important sign of underground oil and natural gas. In the 1930s, geologists began to realize that anticlines are not the only important signs of such deposits of energy resources. *See also* FOLDING; GEOLOGY; PETROLOGY; SYNCLINE.   G.M.B. /W.R.S.

ANTICYCLONE (ant'i sī'klōn') An anticyclone, or high, is a large moving area of high barometric pressure that is marked by clear skies and low humidity. Wind circulates in a clockwise direction around a high-pressure center in the northern hemisphere. In the southern hemisphere, it circulates in a counterclockwise direction.

An anticyclone is the opposite of a cyclone, or low. A cyclone is a large moving area of air that is marked by low barometric pressure, cloudy skies, and precipitation. (*See* CYCLONE.)

Anticyclones move from west to east across the United States. They travel slowly and can remain stationary for several days. Cumulus, or fair-weather clouds, can form in an anticyclone. (*See* CLOUD.) Smog can occur over densely populated areas when winds are too light to blow away exhaust smoke from cars and factories. (*See* SMOG.)

Summer anticyclones in temperate regions feature warm temperatures, clear skies, and light winds. Winter anticyclones have low temperatures, clear skies, and strong winds. A Bermuda high is an anticyclone that affects the eastern part of the United States several

times each summer. It is a stationary high, centered near Bermuda, an island east of North Carolina. The Bermuda high brings warm, humid air from the Caribbean area into the southeastern and eastern states.

Permanent anticyclones can form over land and ocean areas. Much of Siberia is covered by a large anticyclone every winter.

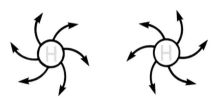

In the diagrams above, the *H* stands for high barometric pressure. Wind circulates around a high-pressure center: clockwise in the northern hemisphere (left) and counterclockwise in the southern hemisphere (right).

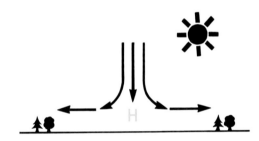

Anticyclones in temperate regions are characterized by sinking air, clear skies, and wind. Again, the *H* stands for high barometric pressure.

The so-called horse latitudes of the oceans, 30°N and 30°S, have permanent anticyclones. They create trade winds, steady breezes that blow in one direction for weeks at a time. When sailing ships were common, they used these winds to cross the oceans. *See also* AIR; WEATHER; WIND.   W.R.P./C.R.

ANTIDOTE *See* POISON.

ANTIFREEZE (ant'i frēz') An antifreeze is a substance that, when added to a liquid, lowers the freezing point of that liquid. The main ingredient of an antifreeze is usually a type of alcohol. (*See* ALCOHOL.)

Ethylene glycol is the basis of the most common antifreeze. It is used in the cooling systems of internal combustion engines, such as those in many automobiles. During the cold winter months, this antifreeze is used alone or with water to prevent the freezing of the cooling system. Methanol is also sometimes used as an antifreeze in internal combustion engines. These antifreezes are often drained out of the cooling system after the threat of freezing is over. Often, because of evaporation, antifreeze loses its power. It can also creep into the block of an engine and cause problems in lubrication.

Ethylene glycol is also used to prevent icing of propellers and wings of airplanes. Glycerol and ethyl alcohol are used to protect drugs and cosmetics from freezing during storage. Calcium chloride and sodium chloride, unlike other antifreezes, are salts used in refrigeration.   J.J.A./J.M.

ANTIGEN *See* ANTIBODY.

ANTIHISTAMINE *See* ALLERGY.

ANTIMATTER (ant′i mat′ər) All matter is made up of very small particles called elementary particles. An elementary particle cannot be broken down into smaller particles, and its size is too small to measure. All elementary particles have a corresponding antiparticle. These antiparticles are almost identical to their ordinary particles. They have the same mass, but some other properties, such as electric charge or spin, are reversed. For example, an electron has a negative charge. Its antiparticle is called a positron, and it has a positive charge. Antiparticles are produced in reactions made by particle accelerators. (*See* ACCELERATORS, PARTICLE.)

Particles and their antiparticles can exist together only for a very short time. The soon collide and destroy each other. Radiation, in the form of gamma rays, is produced in the reaction.

Antiparticles make up antimatter. The big bang theory suggests that the universe was created by a single, large explosion. This explosion could have produced matter and antimatter in equal amounts. The high temperature of such an explosion could have kept the two apart. Then they could have moved to various parts of the universe. There are huge amounts of radiation in the universe. This could be caused by this matter and antimatter coming together. However, nobody knows if this is true or not. *See also* ATOM; COSMOLOGY; PARTICLE PHYSICS.   M.E./J.T.

ANTIMONY *See* ELEMENT.

ANTISEPTIC (ant′ə sep′tik) An antiseptic is a chemical that either kills or stops the growth of microorganisms on living tissue. It is different from a disinfectant, which destroys microorganisms on nonliving objects. (*See* DISINFECTANT; MICROORGANISM.) Antiseptics are used in operating rooms of hospitals to make sure no microorganisms can enter the patients' bodies and cause infection. First-aid medicine includes antiseptics to stop any microorganisms that may be present on the skin around a cut. *See also* ASEPSIS; INFECTION.   S.R.G./J.J.F.; M.H.M.

ANTITOXIN (ant′i täk′sən) Organisms make antitoxins to protect themselves against toxins. A toxin is a chemical that is poisonous to an organism. Most toxins are proteins. Most antitoxins are antibodies, which are also proteins. Certain bacteria, snakes, and other organisms make toxins that are dangerous to humans. For example, the bacteria that cause diphtheria and tetanus produce toxins that can kill a human. The human body produces many antitoxins to neutralize (make harmless) toxins that are produced by disease-causing bacteria. When a person does not have enough antitoxin in his or her blood, a doctor will inject some from another animal to help the person fight the toxins. *See also* ANTIBODY; IMMUNITY.

S.R.G./J.J.F.; M.H.M.

ANTLER Antlers are bone growths from the heads of most male deer and some female deer. The only male deer without antlers are the Chinese water deer and the musk deer. The caribou and reindeer are the only kinds of deer in which both the males and females have antlers. Antlers are used for defense. They are also used during the mating season, when male deer fight head-on for female mates.

Unlike the horns of other animals, deer antlers are solid bone. Horns are hollow, bony growths with a skinlike covering. Antlers are part of the skeleton. Horns are not part of the skeleton.

Deer lose their antlers every spring after mating season. New antlers grow during the summer, fall, and winter months. At first, the new antlers are covered with a velvety tissue. When the antlers are fully developed, this covering dries and cracks. Deer rub their antlers against trees to rid their antlers of this dead tissue.

The moose is the largest member of the deer family. Its antlers sometimes grow to 6 ft.

Antlers grown by deer provide weapons for defense and mating battles. In some species, both females and males grow antlers. In most species of deer, however, only the males grow them. New antlers grow each year, starting in summer. They are shed in the spring.

[1.8 m] in width. Other deer antlers range from short and spiky to long and branched.

In prehistoric times, humans made tools out of antlers. In China, antlers are still used in the making of some medicines.

The size of antlers is usually determined by the age of a deer. When some deer get very old, their antlers become smaller. A deer's health and the environment it lives in also determine the size and condition of its antlers. *See also* DEER.   G.M.B./R.J.B.

ANUS (ā′nəs) The anus is the opening at the lower end of the alimentary canal. All organisms with a complete digestive system have a mouth through which food can be taken and an anus through which solid wastes, called feces, pass from the body. Anal sphincter muscles surround the anus of most animals. These muscles control the release of feces by controlling the opening and closing of the anus. A baby does not have control over the anal sphincter muscles. Control of them is voluntary and must be learned. *See also* ALIMENTARY CANAL; DIGESTION; INTESTINE.

A.J.C./J.J.F.

AORTA (ā ȯrt′ə) The aorta is the largest and longest artery in the human body. It carries oxygen-rich blood away from the heart to the other major arteries. The aorta starts in the left ventricle of the heart and rises to near the bottom of the neck. It then arches backward and downward through the chest and abdomen. Arteries branch off the aorta along its entire length. These arteries supply blood to the heart muscle, the brain, and all other body tissue. *See also* ARTERY; CIRCULATORY SYSTEM; HEART.   A.J.C./J.J.F.

APATITE (ap′ə tīt′) Apatite is a the name for a group of common minerals containing calcium phosphate. Apatite also contains chlorine or fluorine. Its name comes from the Greek word *apate*, meaning "deception." The mineral is well named, as apatite may look like several other minerals. Its crystals may be brown, yellow, green, blue, violet, white, or even colorless. Apatite is found in many kinds of rocks. In North America, Florida is the main source of apatite. Other large deposits are found in the Soviet Union and North Africa.

Apatite has the hardness standard 5 in Mohs scale. (*See* HARDNESS.) Apatite is used in the making of fertilizer and phosphoric acid. *See also* PHOSPHORIC ACID.   J.J.A./R.H.

APE Apes are primates belonging to the family Pongidae. Apes have long arms, fingers, and toes. They have hairy bodies with no

Gorillas (pictured), chimpanzees, orangutans, and gibbons are all apes. In the animal kingdom, apes are probably second in intelligence only to human beings.

tails. Apes have large brains and are probably second in intelligence only to human beings. Apes live in tropical areas of Asia and Africa. The so-called great apes include chimpanzees, gorillas, and orangutans. The smaller, lesser apes include the six kinds of gibbons. Monkeys are different from apes because monkeys have tails and do not walk upright.

Apes look similar to human beings. Apes, though, do not stand completely upright. When they walk, they use their arms and knuckles to help support their weight. *See also* ANTHROPOID. A.J.C./J.J.M.

APHID (ā′fəd) An aphid, or plant louse, is a small, soft-bodied insect that damages plants. The aphid has a needle-shaped mouth that it sticks into a plant. It then sucks out the plant juices. Aphids can often spread disease from one plant to another. Aphids may be any of several colors, but most are green or black. The male usually has four wings. The female is often wingless.

After mating in the fall, the female lays her eggs. These eggs hatch in the spring. The newborn aphids, which are females, then give birth to other living aphids from unfertilized eggs within their own bodies. This form of reproduction, called parthenogenesis, produces many aphids each summer. (*See* PARTHENOGENESIS.)

Some kinds of aphids have a symbiotic relationship with ants. (*See* SYMBIOSIS.) The aphids produce a sweet, waxy fluid called honeydew, which ants like to eat. Ants protect the aphids in exchange for this honeydew.

A.J.C./J.R.

APOLLO PROJECT Apollo (ə päl′ō′) was the name of a large spaceflight project involving thousands of scientists, astronauts, technicians, and manufacturers assembled by NASA (National Aeronautics and Space Administration) in 1961. The aim of the project was to land men on the moon and bring them back safely before 1970. This goal was set by President John F. Kennedy on May 25, 1961, and unanimously approved by Congress.

Apollo beat its deadline by half a year. Civilian Astronaut Neil Armstrong stepped from the lunar module *Eagle* onto the surface of the moon in July, 1969.

At right, aphids feed on a plant. Above is a kind of aphid known as a greenfly.

There were many problems in the early stages of the project. A rocket powerful enough to reach the moon had to be designed and built. New launching, training, and research bases were needed. A worldwide radio tracking network had to be set up.

One of the main functions of the manned trips to the moon was to gather samples and to make measurements of such things as gravity and solar radiation. Here an astronaut on the Apollo 12 mission sets up a solar-powered testing device.

The method chosen for the attempt at landing on the moon was called lunar orbit rendezvous. Three astronauts would travel to the moon in a three-part spacecraft. The crew would live in the command module. The service module would hold necessary equipment. The third part was the lunar module.

The whole spacecraft would orbit, or circle, the moon at great height. Two astronauts would climb into the lunar module (LM) and use it to go down to the surface of the moon. Later, a part of the LM would bring the astronauts back to the command and service modules. The LM would be discarded before the spacecraft returned to earth.

United States Navy divers prepare the Apollo 8 spacecraft for hoisting aboard the U.S.S. Yorktown after landing on December 27, 1968.

On January 27, 1967, Apollo had a serious setback. Astronauts Virgil Grissom, Edward White, and Roger Chaffee were burned to death in a fire aboard the spacecraft during a practice session. The spacecraft had to be redesigned. Flight testing resumed in October, 1968, with the earth-orbital mission, Apollo 7.

During December, 1968, the first flight around the moon took place when astronauts Frank Borman, James Lovell, and William Anders circled the moon ten times, transmitting a special television program on the occasion of Christmas.

On July 20, 1969, Armstrong and Edwin Aldrin landed on the moon in an area known as the Sea of Tranquillity. Michael Collins remained aboard the Apollo 11 command module in orbit. Armstrong and Aldrin stayed on the moon for 21 hours, 35 minutes.

In November, 1969, the Apollo 12 team landed Charles Conrad and Alan Bean on the moon, with Richard Gordon remaining on board the orbiting spacecraft. In April, 1970, an explosion ripped open the service module of Apollo 13 when it was 200,000 mi. [320,000 km] from earth. The crew and spacecraft were successfully brought back to earth.

Astronauts on the Apollo 17 mission in 1972 were aided in their work by the lunar rover seen behind the flag. It allowed them to cover more of the moon's surface than would have been possible by walking. The large device is the lunar module that carried astronauts back and forth from the orbiting command module.

Four successful Apollo moon landings followed. The last three lunar landing missions each carried a battery-powered four-wheeled car, the lunar rover, to let the astronauts do part of their exploring by driving rather than by walking. The final landing, Apollo 17, happened on December 11, 1972. Eugene Cernan and Harrison Schmitt spent 74 hours, 59 minutes on the moon and returned with 250 lb. [113.6 kg] of lunar material, while Ronald Evans stayed in the orbiting command module. *See also* ARMSTRONG, NEIL ALDEN; MOON; SPACE TRAVEL.

W.R.P./J.VP.

APOPLEXY *See* STROKE.

APPENDIX (ə pen′diks) The appendix is a part of the intestines in humans. Its full name is the vermiform appendix. The appendix is found on the lower right side of the abdomen. It is about 1 to 6 in. [2.5 cm to 15.25 cm] in length. The appendix is attached to the cecum. The cecum is the first part of the large intestine.

Although the appendix does not serve a useful purpose today, it was probably a necessary part of the digestive system thousands of years ago. The human diet was different then from what it is now, and digestion of those different foods may have made the appendix necessary. *See also* DIGESTION; INTESTINE.

S.A.B./J.J.F.

APPLE An apple is the fruit of about twenty-five species of trees belonging to the rose family, Rosaceae. (*See* ROSE FAMILY.) There are thousands of kinds of apples in three categories: cooking apples, cider apples, and dessert apples. When ripe, apples are usually red, yellow, or green. They have round shapes and measure 2 to 4 in. [5 to 10 cm] in diameter.

Apples grow in most parts of the United States and the rest of the world. Apple trees require long dormancy, which means that some period of relatively cold weather is needed. Apples cannot usually be grown in tropical places. (*See* DORMANCY.)

Scientists believe the apple originated thousands of years ago in Turkey as the fruit of a wild roselike shrub. Since then, humans have developed that wild plant into the many kinds of apple trees we know today.

Apples contain vitamins A and C. They are good sources of dietary fiber and are high in carbohydrates. G.M.B./T.L.G.; F.W.S.

APRICOT (ap′rə kät′) An apricot is the fruit of a tree belonging to the rose family, Rosaceae. (*See* ROSE FAMILY.) It has a smooth pit

The apricot is believed to have originated in China thousands of years ago. It is a delicious and nourishing fruit, both fresh and dried.

called a stone at its center. It looks like a yellow peach except that its skin is not fuzzy like that of a peach. Apricot trees grow best in fairly warm places. These trees resist drought well. They can live as long as one hundred years.

An apricot can be eaten fresh as a dessert fruit. It also can be preserved by canning or drying. Apricots are a good source of vitamin A. Dried apricots are an excellent source of iron.

Scientists believe the apricot tree originated in China thousands of years ago. Today, it grows throughout the earth's mild climate zones. Spain is the world's leading producer of apricots. Most of the apricots grown in the United States come from California.

G.M.B./F.W.S.

AQUACULTURE *See* AGRICULTURE.

AQUATIC PLANT An aquatic (ə kwät′ik) plant is a plant or plantlike organism that lives in water. It is also called a *hydrophyte,* which means "water plant." There are many different forms of aquatic plants. They may belong to many different divisions of the plant kingdom and other kingdoms. Submerged plants are species that live completely under water. Most of the algae (members of kingdom Monera) are examples of this form. Floating plants float freely on the surface of the water. Duckweed and wolffia are floating plants. Emergent plants have their roots and bases in the water but grow leaves above the water surface. A cattail plant is a tall, emergent plant.

Plants that live in the water must adapt to conditions that do not exist on land. Submerged leaves and stems of aquatic plants do not have a thick, waxy cuticle, or film, to prevent evaporation as land plants do. (*See* LEAF.) Many submerged plants do not have roots. They must absorb water and minerals through the leaf surface. Some algae that are

EXAMPLES OF AQUATIC PLANTS

liverwort

laminaria, a brown seaweed

myriophyllum

duckweed

water lily

Aquatic plants (which include organisms that are plantlike but do not belong to the plant kingdom) are found throughout the world. They grow in both freshwater and marine (seawater) environments.

exposed to the air at low tide are covered with mucus to prevent their drying out.

The pollen of flowering plants on land is spread by wind and insects. (*See* POLLINATION.) This cannot occur with submerged flowering plants. These species have developed methods of underwater pollination.

Aquatic plants are important members of the water environment. They supply food, shelter, and oxygen for many animals. However, if aquatic plants grow too plentiful, they can clog waterways and cause other problems. This overgrowth is usually the result of water pollution.

S.R.G./M.H.S.

AQUEDUCT (ak′wə dəkt′) An aqueduct is an artificial channel that carries water from one place to another. It can consist of a pipeline above or below the ground, a tunnel, or an open ditch. It may also be a bridgelike structure that carries water across a valley. Water moves through an aqueduct either by means of gravity or under pressure from pumps. Aqueducts are used to bring drinking water to cities and irrigation water to farmland. They are also used in hydroelectric projects. (*See* HYDROELECTRIC POWER.)

The aqueducts that are used to bring drinking water to cities can be hundreds of miles long. The Colorado River Aqueduct uses a combination of concrete-lined tunnels and open canals to carry water 242 mi. [389 km] to Los Angeles. The longest aqueduct in the world is the California Aqueduct. It also serves the city of Los Angeles and is 444 mi. [715 km] long.

The Romans built large aqueducts in Europe two thousand years ago. The remains of many of these are still standing. The Pont du Gard aqueduct at Nimes, France, and another at Segovia, Spain, are the best known. *See also* IRRIGATION.　　　W.R.P./R.W.L.

AQUIFER (ak′wə fər) An aquifer is a layer of gravel, sand, or other porous underground rock, such as limestone, in which groundwater passes through and settles. Aquifers are important underground water reservoirs in many areas. Many places get their water from wells that have been drilled down into aquifers.

During the 1980s, scientists began to be concerned about the rising number of aquifers being polluted by chemicals. The sources of these pollutants include landfills, sewage from cities, underground chemical-waste disposal sites, and underground gasoline-storage tanks

ARACHNIDS

Scorpions (top), harvestmen (bottom left), and spiders (bottom right) are all arachnids. Arachnids are a widespread class of arthropods. Many arachnids are helpful to humans because they eat large quantities of insect pests.

that have leaks. Some coastal communities have also seen the contamination by ocean salt of the aquifers from which they draw their water. Ocean water has seeped in because the overdeveloped coastal communities drained most of the fresh water out of the aquifer. In other communities, such as Phoenix and Tucson in Arizona, aquifers are simply drying up because of overuse by heavily populated communities and by farmers. Unless strong regulations are adopted to curb groundwater contamination, the world's supply of safe drinking water will be at risk. *See also* GROUND-WATER; POLLUTION.   P.Q.F./L.W.

ARACHNID (ə rak′nəd) Arachnids are a class of animals in the group of joint-legged creatures called Arthropoda. The arachnids include spiders, harvestmen ("daddy long-legs"), ticks, mites, and scorpions. They have four pairs of legs, two-part bodies, no antennae, and no wings. They also have two small fangs at the front of their heads. Arachnids do not eat solid food. They extract fluids from animals and plants.

Arachnids are sometimes mistaken for insects. There are several differences between insects and arachnids. Arachnids have two more legs than insects. Insects, unlike arachnids, have antennae and often have wings. *See also* ARTHROPODA; INSECT; PARASITE. G.M.B./J.R.

ARBORETUM (är′bə rēt′əm) An arboretum is a garden where woody plants such as trees and shrubs are grown for decorative, educational, or scientific purposes. Arboretums can cover several acres. The first arboretum was founded in France during the mid-1500s. Some of the best-known arboretums in the United States are Brooklyn Botanical Garden (Brooklyn, New York), National Arboretum (Washington, D.C.), and Morton Arboretum (Lisle, Illinois).   S.R.G./T.L.G.; M.H.S.

ARBORVITAE (är′bər vīt′ē) Arborvitae is a common name for a group of evergreen trees that belong to the genus *Thuja* in the cypress family. *Arborvitae* means "tree of life" in Latin. Early European explorers of North America gave the trees this name. When the explorers were visiting the area now known as Canada, they suffered from the disease scurvy. The native Indians made a tea from the arborvitae tree. This tea helped restore the explorers' health. The two North American species of arborvitae are also known as northern white cedar and western red cedar. However, they are not true cedars. True cedars belong to the pine family. *See also* SCURVY.   S.R.G./M.H.S.

ARC, ELECTRIC An electric arc is a curve of light and heat that forms when a strong electric current leaps across a gap between two electrodes. The electrodes are usually metal or carbon. The electric arc is a stream of electrons and ions passing between the electrodes. The arc gives out light and heat because electrons hit molecules of gases in the air between the electrodes.

The light from electric arcs is very bright. Commercially manufactured arc lights give a very white light from an arc between two carbon electrodes. Arc lights have been used in television and film studios and in searchlights.

When an electric arc passes between two electrodes, the electrodes become very hot. Arc furnaces use arcs to melt steel and other metals. Arc welding uses an electric arc to melt and join metals. *See also* ELECTRICITY; ELECTRODE; ELECTRON; IONS AND IONIZATION.

M.E./J.T.

The arch is an important element in many different kinds of buildings. The arches pictured are part of an eighteenth-century monastery in Mexico.

ARCH In construction, an arch is a curved structure built to support weight above an opening. The most common uses for arches are in bridges; in supports for roadways and railroad tracks; and in windows, doorways, and passageways in buildings. Arches can be made of many substances, including stone, steel, concrete, timber, and even aluminum.

The world's oldest arches were built by the ancient Romans. Around 300 B.C., the ancient Romans used the arch to build bridges and aqueducts. The world's longest span of arches is the Bayonne Bridge in New Jersey. The Bayonne Bridge is 1,652 ft. [504 m] long.

Arches can also be built by nature. Natural arches take hundreds and even thousands of years to form. A natural arch is formed when water flows slowly through soil or porous rock that has a harder rock layer above it. The harder rock stays firm, and the soil or porous rock is slowly carried away with the water. Natural Bridges National Monument in Utah features some of the largest sandstone arches in the world. One such arch, Sipapu, is 220 ft. [67 m] high and spans 268 ft. [82 m].

P.W./L.W.

ARCHAEOPTERYX (är′kē äp′tə riks) The *Archaeopteryx* is the earliest known bird. The word *Archaeopteryx* means "ancient wing." The *Archaeopteryx* evolved from reptiles and lived during the time of the dinosaurs, about 140 million years ago. The first fossil remains

The Archaeopteryx is the earliest known bird. Scientists believe that this animal evolved from a small carnivorous (meat-eating) dinosaur.

of an *Archaeopteryx* were found in Germany in the 1800s.

The *Archaeopteryx* was about 20 in. [50.8 cm] long. The *Archaeopteryx* did not fly very well and probably only for short distances. Its wing muscles were not very large. Unlike the *Pterodactylus,* or flying reptile, the *Archaeopteryx* flapped its wings. The *Pterodactylus* was a glider and did not flap its wings.

The skeleton of an *Archaeopteryx* is like the skeleton of a small, carnivorous (meat-eating) dinosaur. Unlike dinosaurs, which had scales, the *Archaeopteryx* had feathers. The *Archaeopteryx* was unlike modern birds because it had teeth, a long tail, and three clawed "fingers" at the end of each of its two wings. The *Archaeopteryx* probably used its fingers and feet for climbing. *See also* DINOSAUR; PTERODACTYLUS.   G.M.B./D.L.G.; L.L.S.

ARCHEGONIUM (är′ki gō′nē əm) An archegonium is the female sex organ in certain plants and plantlike organisms. It is bottle shaped with a long, thin neck. In the base of the archegonium is the egg. The male sex organ, the antheridium, produces a sperm that enters the neck of the archegonium. The sperm travels down into the base where it joins with the egg. The fertilized egg is called a zygote. The zygote will develop into a new organism, which will disperse itself either by developing seeds or spores. *See also* ANTHERIDIUM; REPRODUCTION.   A.J.C./M.J.C.; M.H.S.

ARCHEOLOGY (är′kē äl′ə jē) Archeology is the scientific study of the physical traces of people of the past. It deals with objects made by people and with the remains of people, plants, and animals. These objects and remains often must be dug up from beneath the earth or water. The purpose of archeology is to explain what people were like in the past and how they lived.

Persons who work in archeology are called archeologists. They often have been trained in other sciences, such as anthropology, biology, geology, and zoology, as well. They use picks and shovels as well as microscopes and radioactive testing in their work.

The first thing an archeologist must do is search for the places where people of the past have lived. The archeologist is like a detective who must solve a mystery. He or she searches for camps, houses, villages, and cities that might be buried. An archeologist also explores caves and underground cemeteries.

The things that archeologists find become pieces of a puzzle. They tell a story of the past. All of the puzzle's pieces cannot always be found. Stone and metal objects may be found. The bones of humans and animals are sometimes found. Fossils are often found. (*See* FOSSIL.) Some things, however, are lost to decomposition, or decay. Items made of straw, cloth, or wood are rarely found. Burned wood in the form of charcoal is very valuable to an archeologist. It is wood that has not decomposed, permitting an archeologist to decide the amount of time that has gone by since its origin.

Archeologists carefully study the objects they find. They also make detailed records of where these objects were found and what they look like. Archeologists use these studies to establish information about people who lived hundreds or thousands of years ago. Carvings on pots tell the archeologist about the kind of art people produced. The construction of their houses and the form of their tools and weapons tell about their building and craft-working skills. The bones of animals might tell what kind of food they ate.

This archeologist is searching for the remains of people who roamed across the Shenandoah Valley in Virginia thousands of years ago.

Archeology began in the 1500s, when the people of Europe became interested in the ancient civilizations of Rome, Greece, and Egypt. Thomas Jefferson of the United States studied Indian mounds in Virginia in 1784. His archeology is considered the first to be done in the modern or scientific way. Archeology before that was mainly a hunt for things to sell to museums and collectors. Unscientific archeology of this sort destroyed things that modern archeologists would have saved. Archeologists today are going back over some of the diggings of earlier archeologists to check for mistakes. Since the 1930s, archeology has become a precise science with strict rules and procedures.

Some of the most famous finds of archeology are the Rosetta Stone of Egypt and the Dead Sea Scrolls of Israel. The Rosetta Stone was found in 1799. It was the chief clue to understanding hieroglyphics, which are the symbols of the written language of ancient Egypt. The Dead Sea Scrolls were found in 1947. They are the first known writings of the Bible. In the United States, archeologists are often called to places where construction workers uncover signs of old Indian life. In Central and South America, archeologists have uncovered the ruins of great Indian civilizations.

Modern technology has advanced archeology. Scientists today are able to determine the age of archeological objects by using chemistry and electronics. Some prehistoric objects are tested for radiocarbon, potassium, and argon content. Instruments for measuring these contents can sometimes tell archeologists how many thousands or millions of years the object has been in its present form. *See also* ANTHROPOLOGY; DATING.   G.M.B./S.O.

ARCHEOZOIC ERA (är′kē ə zō′ik er′ə) The Archeozoic era is the period in the earth's history to which the oldest rocks and the earliest known forms of life belong. It followed the Azoic era, which started when the earth was formed. The Archeozoic era ended about 1,850 million years ago, when the Proterozoic era began. Lava rocks from the Archeozoic era, dating from one to two billion years ago, are found all over the world.

During the Archeozoic era, the oldest mountains in North America—the Laurentians in Canada—were formed. Radioactive dating has shown rocks of the Archeozoic era to be at the base of the Adirondacks, the Colorado Rocky Mountains, and in the Grand Canyon.

The first known signs of life on earth, the algae, were found fossilized in Archeozoic rocks in Africa. These fossils are believed to be about 3.5 billion years old. Fossils dating back to about that time have also been found in Australia and North America. *See also* GEOLOGICAL TIME SCALE.   J.J.A./E.W.L; W.R.S.

ARCHERFISH (är′chər fish′) The archerfish is a freshwater fish that belongs to the family Toxotidae. It is found in India and Indonesia. It gets its name from the way it captures food.

The archerfish, found in India and Indonesia, shoots down its prey with a jet of water. The archerfish gets its name from the way it captures food.

The archerfish has a long snout through which it can squirt water. When the fish sees an insect sitting on a leaf above the water, the fish squirts water at the insect. The water knocks the insect into the water. The archerfish then eats the fallen insect. The fish can aim the stream of water remarkably well.

S.R.G./E.C.M.

ARCHIMEDES (about 287-212 B.C.) Archimedes, called the "father of experimental science," was an ancient Greek physicist, mathematician, and inventor. Among other things, Archimedes discovered how to use levers and pulleys to lift heavy objects, such as large ships. He also learned how to pump water uphill by using his invention, Archimedes' screw. In mathematics, he found out how to measure the area of circles and other figures. He worked out a value for pi (π) and came close to inventing calculus.

Archimedes spent most of his life in Syracuse, a city of Sicily, which is an island of Italy. Here he derived the famous Archimedes' principle, which states that when a solid object is immersed in a liquid, it is pushed up in the liquid by a force equal to the weight of the liquid that has been displaced by the object. It is said that Archimedes discovered this principle in a strange way. According to the story, the king of Syracuse asked Archimedes to tell him if his new crown was pure gold. Archimedes thought of a way to test the crown. He had noticed that when he stepped into a full bathtub, the tub overflowed. His body had displaced a certain amount of water. He concluded that a crown of pure gold should displace the same amount of water as a chunk of pure gold weighing the same as the crown. When making the test, he discovered that the crown was not pure gold. The goldsmith had cheated the king.

Archimedes designed war machines for his king. It is said that he invented giant mirrors to focus the sun's rays in order to burn enemy ships attacking Syracuse. Archimedes' genius helped the king hold off his enemies for three years. Archimedes is said to have been killed during the final battle for the city, when the Romans took over Syracuse. *See also* BUOYANCY; RELATIVE DENSITY. J.J.A./D.G.F.

ARCTURUS *See* STAR.

ARGON (är′gän′) Argon is a colorless, odorless gaseous element. Its symbol is Ar. Argon is one of the noble gases. (*See* NOBLE GAS.) This means that it is chemically inactive. It does not combine easily with other elements. Because of this, it is used in electric light bulbs. A more reactive gas would attack the hot filament.

One percent of the air is argon. Argon can be obtained from the air by separating it from the other gases. This is done by liquefying the air. The argon is then separated by distillation. (*See* DISTILLATION.)

Argon has an atomic number of 18 and an atomic weight of 39.95. It boils at -303°F. [-186°C] and melts at -308°F. [-189°C]. It was discovered in 1894 by the British scientists Sir William Ramsay and Lord Rayleigh. *See also* RAMSAY, SIR WILLIAM. M.E./J.R.W.

ARISTOTLE (384-322 B.C.) Aristotle was a Greek philosopher and scientist who developed many ideas about the nature of life and matter. He also wrote on literature, politics, and ethics. He introduced logic, or systematic reasoning, into science. This was important because it allowed scientists to verify, or test the truth of, their ideas by observation. Aristotle did much work in biology and zoology. He was the first person to classify animals on the basis of structure and behavior. Aristotle stated that dolphins are mammals, not fish.

This idea was not believed for hundreds of years, until proven in the 1800s. He also put forward some of the first ideas on human evolution.

Aristotle

Aristotle's theories were widely believed in the Middle Ages. Some of his ideas may have kept science from moving forward during that period. For instance, Aristotle mistakenly thought that heavy objects fall faster than light objects. He also believed that the sun revolved around the earth. In the 1500s and 1600s, scientists such as Newton, Galileo, and Copernicus proved these ideas wrong. *See also* COPERNICUS; GALILEO; NEWTON, SIR ISAAC. W.R.P./D.G.F.

ARITHMETIC Arithmetic is the branch of mathematics that studies numbers and computations performed on numbers, such as addition and subtraction. A young child who counts on his or her fingers is doing arithmetic. The child can see that his or her hands have five fingers each and that each foot has five toes.

It is easy to see if two groups of objects have the same number of features. Match each object in the first group with one from the second. A group of five sheep, the fingers on one hand, and a pile of five marbles all have something in common, which is the number five.

The number of fingers was probably the basis of arithmetic, explaining why number systems often use groups of fives or tens. A simple way of recording numbers may be by using objects such as marbles. This becomes a problem, however, when dealing in large numbers. A better way is to use symbols in place of objects.

One example of an early system of arithmetic is the ancient Roman system. This system was very simple, using only a few symbols. For example, 15 would be written as ten (X) with five (V), or XV. 378 would be written as CCCLXXVIII. However, it was very complicated to multiply and divide using Roman numerals.

Roman numerals	I	V	X	L	C	D	M
Value	1	5	10	50	100	500	1000

The number system we now use comes from the Hindu-Arabic numerals. This system uses the symbols 1, 2, 3, 4, 5, 6, 7, 8, 9, 0. Using these ten numerals, it is possible to write any number by combining the symbols in different ways. The position of the symbol tells whether it is of units, tens, hundreds, and so on. For example, in the number 238, the 8 stands for eight units, the 3 for three tens, and the 2 for two hundreds. A symbol for zero is necessary in order to tell the differences among twenty-three (23), two hundred three (203), and two hundred thirty (230). The development of zero as a placeholder was a major development in the history of numbers.

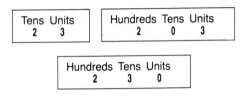

Two groups of things can be combined to make a larger group. When this is done, it is called addition, the basis of arithmetic. Adding can be done by counting the amount of the first number, and then counting on from the first number an amount equal to the second number.

Our system groups numbers in tens. It is possible to add the units together, and then the tens, the hundreds, and so on. The diagram shows what happens when 26 and 38 are added together. The 6 and 8 give a total of 14, or a group of ten and four units. This means a total of six groups of ten altogether, with four more units, written as 64.

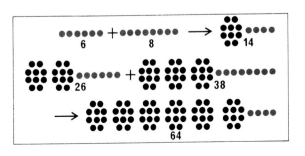

The inverse of addition is subtraction. To subtract one number from another, a person may think in terms of addition. For example, the problem, "What is 8 when 5 is subtracted from it?" may be thought of as, "What number added to 5 gets 8?" The statement 8 - 5 = 3 is true if 3 + 5 = 8.

Multiplying two numbers together may be shown by a process of repeated addition. 5 × 4 means four groups of 5 added together, or 5 + 5 + 5 + 5. This problem may also be seen as five groups of 4 added together, or 4 + 4 + 4 + 4 + 4. Tables for multiplication can be worked out by repeated addition. An easy way to set out the tables is in the form of a square.

X	1	2	3	4	5	6	7	8	9
1	1	2	3	4	5	6	7	8	9
2	2	4	6	8	10	12	14	16	18
3	3	6	9	12	15	18	21	24	27
4	4	8	12	16	20	24	28	32	36
5	5	10	15	20	25	30	35	40	45
6	6	12	18	24	30	36	42	48	54
7	7	14	21	28	35	42	49	56	63
8	8	16	24	32	40	48	56	64	72
9	9	18	27	36	45	54	63	72	81

Square numbers are numbers produced by taking any number and multiplying that number by itself—for example, 1 × 1 = 1, 2 × 2 = 4, 3 × 3 = 9, and 4 × 4 = 16. Square numbers can be shown as sets of dots arranged in squares. An interesting pattern appears in going from one square number to the next.

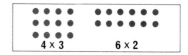

1 = 1
4 = 1 + 3
9 = 1 + 3 + 5
16 = 1 + 3 + 5 + 7

1 + 3 + 5 + 7

The triangular numbers are 1, 3, 6, 10, and so on. It is easy to spot the pattern formed by moving from one triangular number to the next.

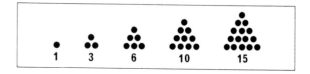

The diagram below shows an interesting connection between the triangular numbers and the square numbers.

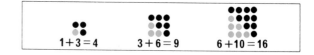

1 + 3 = 4   3 + 6 = 9   6 + 10 = 16

Rectangular numbers can be arranged as a number of equal rows. 12 can be shown as 3 rows of 4 or 2 rows of 6.

4 × 3   6 × 2

Some numbers can be shown only as a single row of dots. These numbers have only 1 and themselves as factors. They are called prime numbers. Whenever a number divides evenly into another number, it is called a factor.

The fourth operation of arithmetic is division. "What is 24 divided by 6?" may be thought of in terms of multiplication, or "What number multiplied by 6 gets 24?"

The numbers used in this discussion of arithmetic were all whole numbers, called positive integers. There are many other kinds of numbers, such as fractions. For example, a cake can be cut into four equal pieces. Each piece is a fraction, or part of, the whole cake. Each piece is one-fourth, written as ¼, of the whole cake.

Another way to write fractions is to use decimal numbers. Decimal numbers are used partly because they are easy to multiply and divide. The fraction ¼ is written as 0.25 when written as a decimal number. The period in a decimal number is called a decimal point.

Mathematicians took centuries to develop the methods now used in arithmetic. Everyone who goes to school learns arithmetic. It is a skill necessary in science, business, and everyday life. Exploring numbers and their various uses can, in itself, be a fascinating study. J.J.A./S.P.A.; R.J.S.

ARMADILLO (är′mə dil′ō′) An armadillo is a mammal belonging to the order Edentata. (*See* MAMMAL.) It has a tough, hard covering that looks like plates of armor. These plates are called scutes. There are twenty kinds of armadillos. They can be found from the southern United States to Argentina. Armadillos are pinkish or brown in color.

Armadillos are mammals that have protective hard plates on their skin.

Armadillos eat insects, spiders, earthworms, and land snails. They have long tongues for licking up their food. They have small teeth at the backs of their mouths. Armadillos cannot bite. They use their strong claws to dig tunnels and burrows in the ground.

The fairy armadillo is about 6 in. [15 cm] long. It is the smallest armadillo. The giant armadillo is about 5 ft. [1.5 m] long. It is the largest armadillo. The nine-banded armadillo is about 2 ft. [60 cm] long. It is the only kind of armadillo found in the United States. It lives chiefly in the most southern states, but scientists say it is moving northward. The nine-banded armadillo gets its name from the nine movable bands of armor on its body. All other kinds of armadillos have three to eighteen movable armor bands on their bodies. The nine-banded armadillo weighs about 15 lb. [6.75 kg]. The female of this species gives birth to four babies, which are always of the same sex.

Some armadillos are killed or trapped because they damage crops. They also damage the foundations of buildings with their underground tunnels and burrows. Armadillos can carry the disease leprosy. Some people eat the armadillo's meat. *See also* LEPROSY.
G.M.B./T.L.G.; J.J.M.

ARMSTRONG, NEIL ALDEN (1930-) Neil Armstrong, an American astronaut, was the first person to set foot on the moon. On July 20, 1969, he and Edwin Aldrin, Jr., landed the Apollo 11 lunar module on the moon. Armstrong was commander of the mission. He stepped onto the moon at 10:56 P.M., eastern daylight savings time. His words, radioed back to earth, were, "That's one small step for man, one giant leap for mankind."

Armstrong was born in Wapakoneta, Ohio. He received a degree in aeronautical engineering from Purdue University. He became a test pilot and flew research airplanes for NASA (National Aeronautics and Space Administration). The rocket-powered X-15 was one of the planes he tested. Armstrong and David R. Scott were the crew of the Gemini 8 flight in March, 1966. The first space docking of two vehicles was made on this flight.

Neil Armstrong

Armstrong resigned from NASA in 1971 and began teaching engineering at the University of Cincinnati. *See also* APOLLO PROJECT.

W.R.P./D.G.F.

ARROW WORM An arrow worm is a small sea creature belonging to the phylum Chaetognatha. It ranges in length from 1 to 4 in. [3 to 10 cm]. Most kinds are transparent. They are found in plankton. Arrow worms live at all depths in the ocean. *See also* PLANKTON.

S.R.G./C.S.H.

ARSENIC (är′sə nik) Arsenic is an element whose symbol is As. Most arsenic compounds are very poisonous. Such compounds are used as insecticides, weed killers, and rat poisons. (*See* COMPOUND; INSECTICIDE; POISON.)

Arsenic has three different crystal forms, called allotropes. (*See* ALLOTROPE.) One of these allotropes, gray arsenic, is the ordinary, stable form. Gray arsenic is metallic. When heated, gray arsenic does not melt. It goes straight from a solid to a gas. This is called sublimation. (*See* SUBLIMATION.) Gray arsenic sublimes at 1,135°F. [613°C]. In nature, arsenic is usually found in combination with sulfur, oxygen, or various metals. The main mineral that contains arsenic is arsenopyrite. Arsenic has an atomic number of 33 and an atomic weight of 74.91.

M.E./J.R.W.

ARTERIOSCLEROSIS (är tir′ē ō sklə rō′səs) Arteriosclerosis is a disease of the arteries, the main blood vessels that supply blood to the tissues of the body. The disease is often called "hardening of the arteries," because it involves hardening, thickening, and loss of elasticity in the artery walls.

There are several kinds of arteriosclerosis. For example, arteriolar sclerosis affects the body's small arteries, called the arterioles. (*See* ARTERY; CIRCULATORY SYSTEM.) The main form of arteriosclerosis is called atherosclerosis. It affects the medium and large arteries. Atherosclerosis has been found in people of all ages, though mostly in middle-aged and older people. The disease tends to develop over a period of years.

Atheroscerosis involves a buildup of fatty material on the inner walls of the arteries. Over time, these deposits enlarge and thicken to form plaques. The plaques, called atheromas, contain calcium, fatty acids, and cholesterol. (*See* CHOLESTEROL.) Atheromas have rough edges that scrape the smooth walls of the arteries. Scar tissue forms. The arteries become hard and narrow, decreasing the flow of blood. The roughened artery walls, together with the slower flow of blood through the arteries, can cause a blood clot to form. If such a clot occurs in an artery that supplies blood to the heart and the artery becomes blocked, the person has a "heart attack." If such a clot occurs in an artery that supplies blood to the brain, a stroke may result. (*See* HEART DISEASE; STROKE.)

For various reasons, physicians do not know for certain how to prevent arterioscle-

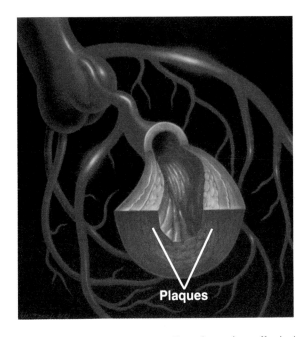

The illustration shows a cross section of an artery affected by atherosclerosis, the main form of arteriosclerosis. Notice the buildup of plaques and how they have narrowed the artery.

Plaques

rosis. For one thing, the disease seems to have no single cause. Also, some of the causes that contribute to the disease—called risk factors—include some that are not preventable. These unpreventable risk factors include a family tendency toward the disease, a person's sex (with males having a greater tendency toward the disease than females), and growing older. However, some risk factors are preventable. One preventable risk factor is high blood cholesterol. A diet that is high in saturated fat (found in foods from animal sources, such as meat, eggs, and dairy products, as well as in tropical oils such as coconut oil) and in cholesterol (found only in foods from animal sources) will increase blood cholesterol in many people. Of these, saturated fat has the greater influence. Therefore, doctors recommend that people limit the amount of saturated fat and cholesterol in their diet. To help prevent arteriosclerosis, doctors also recommend that a person should avoid smoking, get regular exercise, and keep his or her weight within normal limits.

To treat arteriosclerosis once it occurs, doctors also suggest reducing the risk factors. In addition, some patients may take drugs to lower the level of blood cholesterol. In extreme cases, the diseased arteries can be removed and replaced with vessels from other parts of the body or with arteries made of synthetic materials. A less dangerous procedure, called angioplasty, involves inserting a deflated balloon into the artery and inflating it when it reaches the diseased area. This compresses the plaques and allows blood flow to return to normal. *See also* ANGIOPLASTY.

J.J.A./L.V.C.; J.J.F; M.H.M; L.O.S.

ARTERY (ärt′ə rē) An artery is a blood vessel shaped like a tube with thick, elastic, muscular walls. Arteries carry blood away from the heart and to the lungs and the rest of the body. (*See* CIRCULATORY SYSTEM.) The main artery leaving the heart is the aorta, which carries bright red, oxygen-rich blood. (*See* AORTA.) Smaller vessels branch off from the aorta and supply all the organs with blood. Blood returning to the heart contains too little oxygen to meet the body's needs. The pulmonary artery carries this blood to the lungs to pick up oxygen. As the heart pumps, a wave of pressure travels along the walls of the arteries and can be felt as a pulse through the skin over an artery. The smallest arteries are the arterioles. Their walls contract and relax and can regulate the amount of blood flowing to body tissues.   P.G.C./L.V.C.; J.J.F.

ARTESIAN WELL An artesian (är tē′zhən) well is a hole drilled or dug down to underground water. In an artesian well, the water is trapped under great pressure between layers of rock. When the well is drilled, the pressure forces the water up through the hole.

Water can be trapped underground within a layer of porous rock called an aquifer. (*See* AQUIFER.) Sometimes a natural opening allows water from an aquifer to stream out of the ground. This is called an artesian spring.

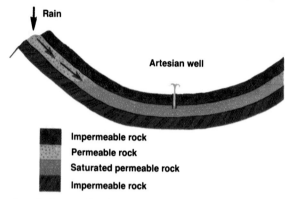

An artesian well is a hole drilled or dug to underground water. In this diagram, the water is in a layer of permeable, or porous, rock between layers of impermeable, or solid, rock.

Some surface water of the Rocky Mountains seeps underground to an aquifer that is called the Dakota sandstone. This aquifer is part of a large geological formation called an artesian basin. Many artesian wells and artesian springs are usually found in an artesian basin. The largest artesian basin in the world is the Great Australian Basin in Australia. *See also* GROUNDWATER; WATER SUPPLY.

G.M.B./W.R.S.

ARTHRITIS (är thrīt′əs) Arthritis is a name for a group of diseases that cause joints in the body to be painful. The term *arthritis* comes from the Greek word meaning "joint inflammation."

People sometimes use the term *rheumatism* to mean arthritis. However, *rheumatism* is actually a more general term that refers to a variety of disorders of the muscles, joints, or connecting tissues, including arthritis.

Arthritis ranges in its severity. The disease can be a minor annoyance, or it can severely cripple a person. Single or multiple joints may be affected. Arthritic joints may become very swollen and crooked. Sometimes these joints become immovable. Although arthritis is more common in older people, it can occur in people of any age. The disease attacks twice as many women as it does men. It is not restricted to humans. The dinosaurs of the Mesozoic era suffered from arthritis.

The exact cause of most kinds of arthritis is not known. Some kinds are caused by injuries or by abnormally high amounts of naturally occurring chemicals in the blood. Some kinds are caused by the wearing away of cartilage over a long life, with first symptoms occurring in old age, or by an allergic reaction to medicine. (*See* ALLERGY.) Some types of arthritis are thought to be caused by infection, most commonly by bacteria or viruses. Other types are thought to be due to the body's immune response to an unknown stimulus.

Scientists have recently discovered a new type of arthritis that is spread to humans by a bite from an infected tick. The disease has been named Lyme arthritis, or Lyme disease, after the town where it was discovered—Lyme, Connecticut. (*See* TICK.) Lyme arthritis is often signaled by a circular rash, which develops at the site of the tick bite.

Arthritis is usually treated with aspirin-type drugs to reduce pain and swelling. Other, stronger drugs, called steroids, are available to control severe pain and swelling for a short period of time. Some people who suffer from arthritis are helped by physical therapy (which includes vigorous body rubs, an exercise program, and sound waves transmitted into the body), supportive equipment, or surgery. *See also* SKELETON.

S.R.G./L.V.C.; J.J.F.